JIM CHRISTY

Rough Road to the North: A Vagabond on the Great Northern Highway is part of the Tramp Lit Series for Feral House. For further information about these titles, see www.feralhouse.com

Front cover top photo: The Alcan Highway from the United States National Archives.

Front cover bottom photo: First truck to go over the rough road along the Alcan Highway, 1942. From the Library of Congress Prints & Photographs Division

Back cover map: Ernie Carter Photographs, 2004-68-54, Alaska and Polar Region Archives, Elmer E. Rasmuson Library, University of Alaska Fairbanks.

 Feral House
1240 W Sims Way #124
Port Townsend WA 98368

Designed by Jacob Covey

ISBN: 9781627310826
Printed in the United States of America
10 9 8 7 6 5 4 3 2 1

ROUGH ROAD TO THE NORTH

JIM CHRISTY

A Vagabond on the
Great Northern Highway

CONTENTS

A Vagabond on the
Great Northern Highway

... the frontier is the wave—the outer edge
between savagery and civilization

Frederick Jackson Turner

1

WHAT IS THE lure of this great land, this ultimate Northwest, Ultima Thule? Something other than the sum of its natural wonder and the drama of its history. There is no other place on earth like it, not even remotely, and if you have spent considerable time here, as have I, it keeps tugging at you when you are gone. It offers, as few other places do, the promise of flat-out old-fashioned adventure. It is inhabited by a kind of people who just do not exist anywhere else. Furthermore, it is heartbreakingly beautiful. It has had its bards but never the epic poet it deserves because before its grandeur and its ferocity one can only be overwhelmed, humbled, silenced. You can live there even now and be a true pioneer, but that will not be true for very much longer—and it is this knowledge too that draws one back, for over this land hangs a vague but palpable melancholy. And through it all winds one road, a lifeline, an achievement of heroic proportions that opened up unlimited potential, brought the world to a few thousand people and revealed a land that since time immemorial had existed in its grandeur and its permanence. The road brought the world, the road brought riches, and the road inevitably cannot but fail to bring the end to a way of life we will never see again.

I have made numerous trips up this Alaska Highway, known also as the Alcan, formerly called the "Road to Tokyo." I have even labored on the road, maintaining it around Whitehorse in the Yukon. So I have lived and worked up here and truly know it well, yet when I am away and begin to think of the land it stirs in me a wanderlust that some might describe—and some do!—as youthful or naïve, but I am a youth no longer. Naïve, yes, in the sense of a wonder one cannot help but feel in the presence of nature. In the sense of the road and its myriad possibilities. "The long brown path before me leading wherever I choose," as Whitman wrote.

I just get to thinking about it. About the cabin I used to have, alone, the only person on Fox Lake in the Yukon and of the lake trout and grayling that were almost too easy to catch. I think of Jesse Starnes, the old prospector in the Peace country. I picture everyone coming in from the bus to spend their dough on a Second Avenue Fairbanks Saturday night. And I think of that Far North road just snaking through the tall trees and bending around the vast cold lakes. And I know I will have to pack up and take off, have to find some excuse to get there; it may be tomorrow or two months from the first time the feeling hits me but I will get there even though it may, and usually does, wreak havoc with any schedule I've set for myself, any projects that have to be completed; even though it might be against good sense, it is unavoidable. The call of the wild.

The feel of that land is always there no matter in what part of the world I might find myself. And it is the part of North America people seem to be most curious about in other countries. The Northwest, Alaska, the Klondike. Not long ago in the airport in Salisbury, Rhodesia, I met a geologist who had just been evacuated from a war-ravaged section of the country near Victoria Falls and he told me his dream was to go hunting for Dall's sheep in the Yukon. I began to talk about the Yukon. How he would have to fly into Whitehorse, hook up with a guide and an outfitter, and charter a bush plane back into the mountains, maybe on the Northwest Territories border near Keele Lake where flying over during hunting season you can see the sheep clinging to the patches of ice on top of the gunmetal-gray mountains. I thought out loud about waking up on those hunting mornings, drinking coffee around the campfire while the wrangler gathers the horses, and then setting off through broad meadows of yellow tundra rose to the foot of high cliffs. I talked about it and he listened and we both dreamed of being there while in the suburbs near the airport the mines of war were exploding. He said he would just have to go and I realized that yet again I would also have to make the long trip. Well, it took me a while to get started but I made it and I hope he did too.

My excuse this time was snow, the cold and the snow. I had never made the entire trip along the Alaska Highway, done all 1,523 miles, when the land, every bit of it, was covered with snow. There would be no tourists, no recreational vehicles raising dust and throwing rocks, the fireplace would be roaring in the 98 Saloon in Whitehorse, the old-timers would be gathered around their barrel stoves spinning yarns and telling lies. It was all the excuse I needed.

I was in the city, Toronto, and the first snow had fallen, the temperature had risen, and it had all turned into slush on the streets and wet dirty drifts at the curb. The city was nearly paralyzed by the paltry snow and people grumbled and complained on the corners and their boots dripped puddles on the dingy subway floor. I told friends I was going up the Alcan and they told me that I was crazy. If these conditions were so miserable, why would anyone knowingly venture farther north, where there was *more* cold and *more* snow? Of course none of them had ever been. It is *different,* I said.

I set about gathering my gear with enthusiasm worthy of one's first big trip away from home. I remembered sneaking out of the house when I was thirteen years old to go off riding freight trains. I remembered that first trip to the Yukon several years before and recalled the nascence of the idea. I was in Toronto then, too, and there was a knock on the door of my room. There was my friend Erling Friis-Baastad and in his hand he held a newspaper clipping. It was about the Yukon, about how the modern world had established itself, yet the people contained within themselves all the spirit of their pioneer heritage. Erling didn't say anything, just held the clipping out to me. I read it and looked at him and he grinned. "Okay," I said, "when do we leave?"

We had both grown up in the States and I believe the lure of the great Northwest is stronger to Americans than Canadians because Americans have always made romance and myth of their history, always pushed on to the frontier. The idea of the frontier, as Frederick Jackson Turner wrote, is "tonic to the people of America." The individual, by conquering the wilderness, thus feels a part of the history of his country. Canadians have stressed the orderly and rational course of events and they seem to turn away from the colorful and chaotic in their past, blushing at the escapades of rapscallions and rodomontades and stress that such are not, ahem, representative of the builders of the nation. To trust Canadian historians one would believe the exploration of the Peace River country and the heady Klondike days to have possessed all the drama of the latest session of Parliament in Ottawa. Had that area been a part of the United States, its lore would be an inherent part of the racial psychology of the nation. Names that are mere footnotes in Canadian history would be folk heroes in America. George Woodcock has noted that Canada is the only country in the world that would make Louis Riel a hero instead of Gabriel Dumont. Of course the larger-than-life figures of the Far North would all have had distorted versions of their lives broadcast week after week on television. How could Wyatt Earp, a quiet saloonkeeper in Nome, Alaska, have ever dreamed that sixty years hence he would be visiting millions of North American living rooms every Wednesday night?

But because the deeds of explorers and adventurers, of pioneers and outlaws, are not part of the fabric of Canadian life, there are open to Canadian historians rich new fields for exploration. An entire alternate history. An uncoopted history. While political events were progressing and being recorded by the official historians, these pioneers were living the actual human history.

Both Erling and I as children in the lower forty-eight had listened to the once-weekly nighttime serialized adventures of Sergeant Preston of the Yukon and his German shepherd dog King. Although we didn't know each other then, we later discovered we had lain in bed listening as Sergeant Preston of the Northwest Mounted Police chased wrongdoers over the frozen barrens with King at the head of the team of huskies. He found murderers knocking back drinks of evil whiskey in murderous saloons, tracked down trappers berserk with cabin fever, saved helpless Indians from the evil machinations of dastardly swindlers who would do them out of their valuable claims.

I can still remember the sound the wind made as some cabin door opened and Sergeant Preston walked in and stomped his boots free of snow. I went to the Yukon only partly because of the wilderness, only partly because of the pioneering spirit. I went to the Yukon, goddamn it, because of Sergeant Preston! And so did Erling.

That article had mentioned the Taku Lounge in Whitehorse, and for lack of any other landmark or reference point we decided to meet in three weeks at the bar of the Taku. Erling left first, it being incumbent upon him to get a job immediately in order to send for his wife Patti.

I took the train to Edmonton and decided to hitchhike out of town, journeying overland like so many did during the Gold Rush. After several rides I made the Yellowhead Route where there was a sign noting this was the road to the Alcan, "a symbol of cooperation between the U.S. and Canada." I made Grande Prairie at midnight and couldn't get a ride so at three forty-five in the morning I bought a bus ticket to Whitehorse.

Not only do Canadians turn away from the Yukon, which is their finest claim on the pageantry of history, but also many of them don't even know where it is. I have gotten letters up there from people Outside addressed to me in Whitehorse, Alaska. The bus station clerk in Grande Prairie made my ticket out for Whitehorse, N.W.T.

The bus arrived in Dawson Creek, Mile 0, of the Alaska Highway at dawn and having six hours to kill I shouldered my pack and went around the corner to the Windsor Hotel for a couple of hours' sleep. Later, on the bus, I stared out the window at the flat snow-covered country, crossed the Peace River at Taylor and, according to my journal of that first trip, wondered "what indomitable purpose it must take to live here winter after desolate winter."

I remember the people on the bus. A guy from France flirting with all the women passengers when he wasn't taking pictures of everything out the window with his expensive Hasselblad. Two girls going to work in cocktail bars somewhere, anywhere, they didn't know exactly, but they had heard there was big money tossed around in the watering holes of the North. There was a white-haired, sincere, and robust Quaker lady who was going to Fairbanks to work as a chambermaid. There were silent Indian women. We stopped for dinner at a Fort Nelson truck stop filled with big men eating huge meals. The waitress was a beautiful country girl with teased hair, stiff new jeans, tooled boots, a western shirt, and she kidded with all the drivers.

Then suddenly the scenery changed, the mountains began, looming beyond the woods in endless ranges white and shadowy in the twilight. Here finally was my dream of the North and I stayed awake long into the night wanting to see the sign that announced YUKON but I fell asleep and missed it, woke as the bus stopped at Rancheria. I stepped outside and breathed the cold mountain air, great gulps to clear my lungs of the city. A Lyndon Transport truck with chrome stacks bound for Anchorage stood on the gravel lot and the driver was inside drinking coffee and eating cinnamon rolls, which I discovered on so many other trips are a Rancheria specialty. Later at Johnsons Crossing I drank more coffee around a potbellied stove with a young Indian kid in a baseball cap who answered patiently my dumb, excited questions about his hometown of Whitehorse.

Finally there was McCrae's roadhouse, the Whitehorse airport, and Two Mile Hill down to the town past garages and the A and W, insul brick Indian homes, and the crumbling dimly lit Greyhound station. I got off, shouldered my pack, and walked through the morning's powdery snow until I found the Taku Lounge at nine in the morning. And there was Erling in his new western gear. He had already gotten a job working on an explosives truck that supplied area mines. We had a drink to celebrate; more than one if the truth be known.

When I had left the flat forested lands behind and for the first time beheld those rugged northern Rockies I felt a wild exhilaration, a feeling that had come to me before and always while traveling, but never had the sheer presence of nature's splendor done it to me. It had always been the anticipation of action, of involvement, people to mingle with, things to see and do. I had viewed the giant muddy swath the Amazon cut through the vast green jungle from fifteen thousand feet and descending, but it was the knowledge that it was the actual Amazon, great river of mystery and history, the *idea* of the Amazon that stirred me.

The feeling was the same but my runaway imagination had gotten me going. As it had before. Only a few times but enough to make travel worthwhile and exciting, and it is those reckless moments remembered that makes one ready to take off again. No matter that everything might have turned out awful, hideous, absurd or downright boring, the remembering mind is selective; mine latches onto those few times.

On the first occasion I was twelve years old, had run away from home, and woke on an early September morning wondering where the hell I was. It happened I was in back of a service station on the turnpike somewhere in western Pennsylvania. There was the forest in back of me, the rolling Alleghenies, the big highway with hundreds of cars rushing back and forth. I jumped up anxious to go, no matter I had no money for breakfast, so what, everything will work out. And it did.

Many years later, in Barcelona, I had a train ticket to Algeciras. I was going to Tangier—Morocco, the Casbah—and I had a couple of hours to kill so I drank wine in a bar near the station. A rowdy raucous place filled with prostitutes and a few of their pimps; old ladies came in to sell thin long sticks of crusty bread and plaster statuettes of saints. The girls were taking a breather before going out to meet the trains. No one bothered them. One sat on a stool, unrolled her stockings, and massaged her feet, and next to her an old man never looked but sipped his dark thick wine and read the sporting papers. That bar in Barcelona seemed literally to vibrate with human hopeful activity and outside on the cobblestoned streets the old-time trolley inched along and people went about their business and you could hear the trains turning in the grimy stone roundhouse.

There was a place to go, something to do, but when I saw that Far North land I was captured by its very presence and suddenly there didn't have to be anything to do and whatever I did would be just fine. Being there and knowing the mountains and the forests were all around were what mattered.

My first time in Whitehorse I got a job in a couple of days with a small construction company and each day found myself on a different site at a different task. One day I would be building a stone fence around a property in the town, the next found me out by the dam on the river driving a tractor, later in the week I was on the highway hauling some timber from the roadside; every so often I would stop and for no particular reason look around me and there was Grey Mountain in the distance. Always there looking down on the highway sneaking through the forests, the river glittering in the sunlight, looming over the streets of small houses. Grey Mountain. It never failed to bring me up full stop in awe and I would wonder why it had taken me so long to get here.

Sure I left, but perhaps because I did and because I always return, the impact is never lost. That first stay though I kicked myself for being late. Everything has its reason, of course, yet I certainly sometimes bemoaned the days I threw away in cities and petty struggles while I could have been up there wandering free. What a life there is to be led there and maybe, too, I feel that way because I know it is not exactly my type of life or at least it suits only part of my disjointed personality. Nevertheless, in that northern land you are able to do as you please and I could imagine myself, or another me, going up there and living the way one can't in any other part of the world. Even on my last trip I had to shake my head to think of all the unemployed in the cities, or worse the young men toiling in factories or at dumb dead-end jobs for ridiculous wages when up there you can work and get paid for it and try your hand at something else if you wish. It is a place that nurtures versatility and gives dimension to men's lives. You meet guys who have been bush pilots, worked as horse wranglers, driven trucks, trapped a few seasons, and next year are going to turn their hand to something new. Men who can seemingly do anything and women who wear independence naturally, they grew up with it by making do and being at ease with their world, and didn't get it from a book as if one day after much study, worry, and meditation came to the conclusion that they were second-class citizens and the situation had to change. It is as if everyone has a place in the scheme of things, yet there are no rigid boundaries keeping them within the confines of some predetermined role. There is an ease to people in the Far Northwest yet a toughness also that one does not find elsewhere. I sincerely believe that the wonderful thing about that country is that one can lead a life that is full and dignified, something that should be everyone's birthright but yet is becoming increasingly difficult if not impossible in the world today, a world that mitigates against such a thing at every turn and is forever devising new ways to crush the human spirit.

AND HERE I WAS eight years later haunting the second-hand stores of Toronto's Queen Street West for lined boots and woolen socks, mittens, and used parkas with all the expectations of that first journey. I wasn't going to waste any time. I wanted to leave the city and all the Outside behind as quickly as possible, so I flew to Dawson Creek. Anxious to get on the road, the wild meandering road that had inspired one local to wonder "whether the dude who built it was going to hell or coming out."

And it is 1,523 miles of *bad* road. Cut and hacked through seemingly impenetrable bush, blasted through moraines laid down over the muck, mire morass of muskeg, spanning glacial rivers, wrapped like a frivolous ribbon around the sides of mountains. Sometimes, looking off into the distance from a promontory, it appears to be nothing more than a crazy unfinished idea, bureaucracy's folly.

Yet when they started putting that road through, it was an idea long overdue. People had been talking about it for fifty years but nothing much was done; yet, when the Second World War broke out, the absence of any road to the Far Northwest seemed like a gross, horrible oversight. When the Japanese bombed Pearl Harbor on December 7, 1941, Americans and Canadians realized the northern part of their continent was virtually unprotected. The day after Pearl, General Simon Bolivar Buckner of the Alaskan Defense Command was to write: "At dawn this morning I watched our entire Alaska Air Force take to the air so as not to be caught on the field. This force consisted of six obsolescent medium bombers and twelve obsolete pursuit planes."

The only ground protection from Vancouver to the Bering Strait was a cannon that sat on the lawn of the capitol building in Juneau facing the sea and which was used as a flower pot.

Two months later, troop trains were rumbling out of Edmonton filled with raw young recruits who had never been in the cold. Thousands of them, and they were to be led by hundreds of officers who had never been in the cold. Few had seen wilderness this dense, mountains this high, or mountains at all. How many had even heard of glaciers or seen an Indian, a trapper, or a guide? Not long ago many of the young men had been loitering about sleepy town squares in Georgia, eating chitlins and ham steak with gravy over grits in their mothers' kitchens by the wood stove, and now they were going out into that awesome cold, and if they were lucky, a local trapper would fix them up some bannock since the supplies wouldn't always get through. Bannock and tea—tea!—at forty below. And how do you fix a carburetor at forty below? How do you raise a two-ton earth mover out of a quagmire peat-bog sea of springtime mud? How do you build a bridge across a river eighteen hundred feet wide when you can't sink pilings because the steel shatters on the riverbed, which is ice and always has been? For that matter, how do you get the equipment in there in the first place?

But these were obstacles that had to be overcome; what were they really when freedom was at stake? But three months into construction, they still seemed insurmountable and back home the cynics and the shirkers were saying it could never be done. All doubts were vanquished and the building of the road was spurred on when the Japanese launched a carrier-based attack on June 3, 1942, against the U.S. Naval Base at Dutch Harbor in the Aleutians. The attack was repulsed by aircraft stationed at Iliamna and Cold Bay but the Japanese captured the Outer Islands, Attu, Agattu and Kiska. Now the road had to go through.

Imagine the scene when the first trains rolled into Dawson Creek, turning that sleepy board sidewalk farming burg into a boom town. Suddenly the whole countryside was transformed. American troops were on active duty on Canadian soil for the first time since 1812. Everything moved with the dynamism of purpose and patriotism. Official proclamation from the town fathers to the U.S. Army: "Dawson Creek on behalf of the forces of democracy welcomes you!"

Orders were given. Men and equipment got into gear. Convoys moved out. There was a frantic hustle of activity and men and women played just as hard. At night they jitterbugged in Quonset huts on the edge of town. There was wartime romance.

It was like a movie of the time. Black and white. 1942. All the characters were there. There was the tough, up-from-the-ranks major of the engineers who would bestir himself from in front of a map with a swarm of pins indicating the progress of the road and the position of the Japs, to go out in the field and take care of an impossible problem. John Wayne. With him in his Jeep was his adjutant, Robert Stack, who knew the old man was a gruff bastard but loved him and respected him and asked, "How high?" when he said, "Jump!" They would arrive at some muddy scene with tractors and Cats and earth movers stuck in the mud and there would be the sergeant from Brooklyn Ernest Borgnine reporting on the situation and whispering that he thought he had seen Jap bombers overhead at dawn. John Wayne would address the men and inspire them with the reminder: "We're the fighting 18th, aren't we? And we're gonna get this road through. We're gonna slap a dirty Jap and go on over and drop a bomb on Hirohito's lap. Unless, that is, you want to go home to Ioway, and take orders from a little slanty-eyed yellow fellow!"

And they put through nine miles of road *that* day!

Meanwhile peering out from the bush in camouflage uniform is Toshiro Mifune, who leers cynically.

Back at headquarters mess the RCAF flier, Errol Flynn, is about to take off on a dangerous mission along the Northwest Staging Route. The weather has just turned nasty but he is not worried, he has that old Canuck *sang-froid* and the air of gallant melancholy with which he charms Olivia de Havilland, who dishes out the chow.

Back in town, his pack horses tied up around back, Gabby Hayes is having a drink in the saloon, the crusty old curmudgeon, the grizzled prospector is entertaining his cronies, other bewhiskered old-timers, with tales of the naïve Yanks out on the highway.

Peter Lorre the German spy is snooping around hotel lobbies taking shorthand notes from behind potted palms.

At night those naïve Yanks, the GI Joes, teach tricks to a malamute pup they've adopted and shoot craps against a wall festooned with postcards from home and pinups of satiny Rhonda Fleming, the back view of Betty Grable.

That road's gonna go through, brother, as sure as there's corn in Iowa and Dodgers in Flatbush.

ON FEBRUARY 2, 1942, a Special Cabinet Committee appointed by President Franklin Delano Roosevelt ordered General R.W. Crawford to report in one week on road-building problems and construction equipment available for establishing a route to Alaska from Edmonton, Alberta. Crawford passed the orders along to Brigadier General C.L. Sturdevant, assistant chief of engineers. Sturdevant quickly devised a plan, which he discussed with officials at the Public Roads Administration (PRA) and got back to the War Department in just two days.

Sturdevant's plan was to have all necessary arrangements made with the Canadian Government, and an allotment from the President's Emergency Fund. There would be two distinct stages in the construction of the highway. The first stage called for the cutting of a pioneer road that "need be sufficient only to get equipment through and to permit troop supply." The second stage would make improvements, build permanent bridges, and theoretically use the pioneer route as a tote road in the building of an all-year-round highway.

On February 6, the plan passed General George Marshall and Secretary of War Henry Stimson, and the President approved it February 11 authorizing Sturdevant to proceed. The responsibilities of the two governments remained to be spelled out but on February 7 FDR had held a press conference in which he profoundly shocked Canadians. He had stated he could give no assurance that the Japanese would not attack Alaska. His words had the effect of illuminating Canada's vulnerability in the West, particularly since all its military might was centered on the European Theater. The Dominion realized then that the road was a necessity and agreements but a formality.

Basically America agreed to conduct surveys to determine the route and to build the pioneer road. It was to order the PRA to prepare building contracts without consideration of whether contractors were Canadians or Americans. Americans were also to maintain the road until six months after the war was over and at such time "transfer that part of the highway which lies in Canada to Canada… subject to the understanding that there shall at no time be imposed any discriminatory conditions" upon the use of the road by Americans.

Prime Minister Mackenzie King agreed to waive all duties, taxes, and license fees on all equipment and supplies used by Americans and on personal effects and to allow use of local timber, gravel, rocks in construction.

Sturdevant's plan also spelled out the roles of the Army and the PRA. The Army was to cut the road and the PRA to follow, correcting grade and alignment, building permanent bridges, and putting down gravel. It was the responsibility of the PRA to employ and manage the private contractors for this work.

The survey for the pioneer route was to be carried out by both Army and PRA crews and the territory was to be divided between them. They both used local guides, mushers, packers, prospectors, and bush pilots to determine the route. When there were disagreements between Army and PRA people—and there were plenty—the Army was to prevail. There was also to be dispute about the quality of the road-building. The PRA consisted of professional road-builders concerned with easy curves and gradual gradients, and the Army had to force them to lower their standards to get the pioneer road through on schedule.

The general's plan also optimistically called for "blacktop or other surface to be added after proper settlement."

The rush to Dawson Creek began. The March 5 edition of the Peace River *Block News* announced that in just a couple of days their old town would be unrecognizable. "Staff headquarters will be in the 3 story building formerly the 'Five to a Dollar Store' owned by Harry Brown."

So it was that on the morning of March 9 while the temperature stood at thirty below the three hundred inhabitants of Dawson Creek were awakened by the sound of the first train carrying Captain Elmo Schly of Green Bay, Wisconsin; G.W. Happle of Lubbock, Texas; E.C. Winters of Bellingham, Washington; and ninety-one enlisted men of the U.S. Quartermaster Corps who would establish camp "on George Chamberlin's spread west of town."

The army had arrived. Dawson Creek had arrived unto the modern world. Soon, just beyond the railhead, the silence that had lasted forever would be shattered by the roar of diesel Cats.

Advise go by way of Skagway.

Inspector Moodie,
NWMP

2

ALTHOUGH THE AMERICAN Army came and built the Alcan, they were not the first to dream of a road that would connect Alaska with the mainland, nor were they even the first to begin building. Such a project had long excited men's imagination. The desirability of an international route was impressed upon the stampeders when gold was discovered on Bonanza Creek, formerly Rabbit Creek, near Dawson City in 1897.

There were three main routes to the gold fields, each very long and very costly and, of course, the least expensive was the most arduous. One way was by ship all the way to the mouth of the Yukon River on the Bering Sea, and from there upriver by steamboat to Dawson City, over a thousand miles away. That was the easiest and most expensive route. It was the lack of any money at all that had inspired most stampeders to head for the gold fields. If they had possessed the money for such a long boat ride they probably wouldn't have felt the need to leave their homes. Most stampeders therefore made it to Skagway and carried their supplies over the Chilkoot or the White Pass to Whitehorse and then three hundred miles downriver to Dawson. Some traveled to Edmonton and followed the rivers to Great Slave Lake, steamered down the Mackenzie and crossed the mountains into the Yukon. This was the compromise route, almost as long as the first and almost as arduous as the second. It was the cheapest, the road that beckoned the drifters and no-accounts. It was called "The poor man's route to the Yukon" and "the back door to the Klondike."

The Gold Rush made Edmonton. Commerce boomed as would-be prospectors arrived thinking they might walk to the gold fields and pick up nuggets on the creekbeds. They would walk down Main Street, see the bush that was to stretch for another eighteen hundred miles to Dawson, and turn around and come back to town. Evidently the first person to attempt to blaze an overland trail was a local prospector who should have known better. Dan Noyes was a well-known old-timer. He grandly formed the Alaska Mining and Transportation Company and announced that he would build a stagecoach road to Alaska complete with a system of five ferries and a series of fine hotels along the way. Nothing came of his scheme, however, and he had to give back all the advance subscriptions he had garnered from the Outsiders with no experience of the North, the cheechakos.

Noyes' dream must have attracted the attention of the Northwest Mounted Police, because their Inspector Moodie was soon instructed "to leave Edmonton for the headwaters of the Pelly River, the object being to collect exhaustive information on the best road to take parties going into the Yukon via that route, and with this object in view you must map out the route and carefully work the portion over which a wagon road can be made without expense and you must note the supply of fuel, feed and hay... remember that the object is to find a horse and cattle track where a wagon road is possible."

How casually this immense task was laid at Moodie's feet. Make this epic journey and see to it a road can be built with no expense. How typical of the Mounted. It would not have fazed Preston and it did not faze Moodie. Picture him with a click of boot heels, a nod, and a salute, leaving headquarters and setting forth immediately. The incredible thing is that he did it. It took him from September 4, 1897, to November 7, 1898—fourteen months—but he blazed his trail to Fort Selkirk in the Yukon. It was a heroic achievement. Consider that three thousand gold seekers followed him and only ten arrived at Selkirk.

It was in his report to headquarters that Moodie drily noted, "Advise go by way of Skagway."

His report was consigned to the files and not found until 1905, when the NWMP decided to make a road eight feet wide, passable for wagons, with rest houses every thirty miles. Moodie's trail had long grown over, so it was a fresh task for the NWMP party. On St. Patrick's Day 1905, Inspectors Constantine and Richards, Sergeant Wilson, and Constable Thorne, along with thirty-two other men, set out from Fort St. John. By the fall of 1907 they had reached the Yukon Telegraph Line 104 miles north of Hazleton, British Columbia. They had built 380 miles of road, eight feet wide, and the next year, when winter was done, planned to carry on to Dawson City. But there was to be no next year. The government, for no particular reason, as governments are wont to do, changed its mind.

During the first decade of the century the initial nongovernmental proposals were introduced to link eastern Canada with Alaska. The Toronto *Globe* was then the prime protagonist of national expansion and pushed a scheme for a railroad from Toronto to the Yukon and the Bering Strait. The *Globe* idea inspired Edward H. Harriman, father of Averell Harriman, who wanted to continue his Union Pacific Railway not only to the Bering Strait but through it by tunnel to meet the Trans-Siberian Railway.

The idea for a road to Alaska was reborn in the late 1920s when international highway associations were formed in Fairbanks and Dawson City. The Alaska Legislature adopted the project officially on April 17, 1929, but it foundered until 1931, when the Alaska Road Commission conducted a survey to determine the best road from the southern Yukon to Fairbanks. Donald MacDonald, an American engineer, headed the team and cut a trail over the entire distance to prove that a road could be established. An Alaska University student named Ed Borders made a midwinter snowshoe journey over the route to demonstrate its feasibility. MacDonald suggested the United States send its Depression unemployed to build the road. The government was not interested.

In Canada, the idea for an international highway had only one public promoter in the early thirties, and that was the premier of British Columbia, Simon Fraser Tolmie. The premier and various businessmen organized car caravans to the north of their province to publicize the Pacific Yukon Highway.

American General William "Billy" Mitchell had long been trying to call the attention of his government to the strategic importance of the Aleutians. He frequently cited a book by General Herman Lea, published after the Boxer Rebellion, that clearly outlined Japanese military intentions. Mitchell likened the Tanaka Memorial to Hitler's *Mein Kampf.* The Tanaka Memorial of 1927 was the progeny of Foreign Minister Tanaka, and it expounded the military aspect of Japan's destiny. It was in reality a manifesto of conquest. Mitchell stressed that a road to Alaska was absolutely necessary for the protection of North America's Pacific Coast. He was alone in urging that an international highway be built for military rather than economic reasons. But the Yankee Giant, blue-eyed Uncle Sam, slumbered on in isolationism. And Canadians, as historian Donald Creighton would later note, are "a profoundly unmilitary people." They also slept snug in the blanket of neutrality.

Although no one in Canada took notice of the Dominion's military weakness in the Northwest, it feared the United States wanted to strengthen its own position. As the different American-oriented plans for a road emerged, Canada viewed each as a plot for its own military domination. Actually, what Canada did not seem to realize was that the result of these American schemes would have led to economic domination even if they weren't designed with such outright motives. It is typical that America acted with insensitivity and Canada responded with paranoia.

In 1932 a group of Seattle businessmen attempted to finance the building of an Alaskan highway. Their plan was to build the highway with their own money in exchange for hotel and gasoline concessions in Canada.

In 1933 President Hoover's Alaska Highway Commission investigated the practicability of such a route but did so without Canadian cooperation. Their finding was that an international highway would cost the United States two million dollars and Canada twelve million!

The Chief of the Canadian General Staff, Major General E.C. Ashton, reported to the Minister of National Defense that the proposed highway was really "a military project engendered by the U.S. fear of Japanese aggression." So would Billy Mitchell have wished.

Ironically, it was not until the eve of Pearl Harbor that the American military expressed any interest at all in a land route to Alaska. As late as August 1940, Secretary of War Stimson was to say, "The value of the proposed highway as defense measure is negligible."

Meanwhile few Canadians were expressing interest in such a road and most who even considered the notion deemed its construction impossible. Even while it was being built, Canadians in official positions would express their doubts, as did the British Columbia minister of education, H.G. Perry, who warned that the entire project was "a grave mistake."

One man who disagreed with him was his own premier, T.D. Patullo, whose enthusiasm over the economic benefits of an Alaskan highway led to an embarrassing incident. Unable to secure financing in British Columbia or to rouse any interest in Ottawa, Patullo approached the United States for assistance. When the United States proved willing to listen, Patullo without clearing his actions through Ottawa actually went down to Washington, hat in hand, to ask for a loan. The Canadian Government was incensed at Patullo's going over their heads and getting involved in international affairs, which they were quick to remind him are not exactly the responsibility of a provincial premier.

So Patullo was virtually alone in Canada save for the rare editorial writer. One such anonymous journalist on a small prairie weekly compared an Alaskan highway in Canadian history to the Canadian Pacific Railway. Both were based on military needs, he rightly claimed. The CPR was built partly as a British imperial lifeline in the event of war with Czarist Russia. The Alcan would be built for both offensive and defensive action against Japan. The CPR had brought about and the Alcan would bring about settlement of vast un-peopled areas, the opening of resources, the development of travel and tourism. But this journalist's vision was a lone wind whistling on the prairies. The pioneering spirit had not developed the Dominion of Canada. It did, however, have a firm hold on the being that was Charles E. Bedaux.

The name of Charles Bedaux is not known these days but in the thirties and forties he was notorious: as the scourge of labor and a collaborator of the Vichy and Nan governments. He made society headlines when the Duke of Windsor and Wallis Warfield Simpson were married at his one-thousand-acre estate in the Touraine.

In Canada there exist but four chapters on Charles Bedaux. In the forties a former fur trader and retired Army officer, Philip Godsell, sketched Bedaux's Canadian adventures in his book about the Northwest. He added his memories of Bedaux's activities to an outline of facts provided by an article in the *Canadian Geographical Journal*. In the seventies Pierre Berton, having pillaged a 1956 *Maclean's* magazine article by Mackenzie Porter, poked fun at Bedaux in his book *My Country: the Remarkable Past*. Both men might have looked a little farther.

The reason they chose to write about Bedaux is because he came to Canada to attempt to blaze a trail to Telegraph Creek in the Yukon from the Peace River country. Both Berton and Godsell conclude that Bedaux was a bumbling inept and both reveal the existence of his salient international connections. Godsell makes no comment on the significance of Bedaux's exploring the country later traversed by the Alaska Highway. Berton dismisses the espionage factor: "...the real explanation, surely, is simpler," he concluded; Bedaux "...was exactly what he claimed to be: a rich nut ... a self-made success squandering his funds on a fantasy ... a five-foot-six egotist trying desperately and not very effectively to be noticed."

But Charles Bedaux despite his diminutive stature never had trouble being noticed, and more than once demonstrated his ability to turn his "fantasies" into reality. Bedaux was never to fail in any of his far-flung enterprises and he did not fail in Canada.

But who was this shadowy figure? "The son of an impoverished French railroad worker," wrote Berton. Actually he was of middle-class origins, born in 1887 in the Paris suburb of Charenton. His brother was a professor of mathematics at the Sorbonne but Charles denounced his background and set sail, steerage class, for America in 1906, arriving penniless. He drifted from job to job, working in New York as a laborer on the East River Tunnel and as a pearl diver in a Bowery saloon. He returned to France to fight in the First World War but came back to New York and became a naturalized citizen in 1917. While working for the Mallinckrodt Chemical Works he brought his pet efficiency scheme to the attention of his employers who let him try it out on the company. It worked. Bedaux quit, wrote a novel to popularize his system, and set up business for himself.

The system was a wage incentive plan using "Bedaux units" to measure human productivity, one unit indicating the work to be done by one person in one minute. A bonus was due for work done in excess of sixty units per hour. The plan increased production and stimulated management efficiency but labor claimed it was nothing more than an insidiously disguised speed-up scheme.

General Electric soon offered to buy his entire system, his records and staff. Bedaux refused to sell and thereby gained even more notoriety in industrial and commercial circles. Bedaux, from his headquarters in the Chrysler Building, dispatched his efficiency experts to offices and factories throughout the world.

Bedaux opened offices in the far corners of the globe. He purchased his French chateau and a grouse-shooting lodge in Scotland. Bedaux maintained an estate in Hungary which he used two weeks a year for wild boar hunts. (The houses and grounds, it must be noted, are now occupied by socialist mental patients.) He became fabulously wealthy. He was a shining controversial star in the glamorous firmament of capitalistic modernism.

But Bedaux was forever leaving his business enterprises to go on curious expeditions. When Citroën launched the first successful attempt to cross the Sahara in motorized vehicles—Caterpillar tractors—Bedaux responded that he could cross with passenger automobiles. He did. With five Citroëns rigged with tractor tread tires. Then he disappeared in the mountains of Asia. But the interest of the Canadian writers does not begin until Bedaux appears in Fort St. John, British Columbia, in September 1934, to lead an expedition of Citroën tractors across the wilderness to the Yukon.

Godsell calls attention to Bedaux's total lack of experience in the Canadian wilds and Berton cynically chronicles the expedition's stores: "There was champagne of course, cases of it . . . pâté de foie gras and caviar, truffles and chicken livers, Devonshire cream and candied fruits ... nests of French cooking pots, rugs and cashmere sweaters, tropical suits ..." etc.

Curiously, two years before this Bedaux expedition into northern British Columbia, a local newspaper, the Peace River *Block News*, on September 16, 1932, carried the headline: "French Hunting Party Largest Ever to Leave Hudson Hope." It was Bedaux's party and it was guided by J.B. Bocock of Edmonton. The article mentions farther on that Bedaux had made a similar trip to British Columbia the previous year with a local woodsman, R.C. McCorkell of Vanderhoof. Even earlier visits were made by Bedaux, in 1929 and 1926! The 1932 party was ostensibly a hunting party and Bedaux did shoot the largest moose ever taken in the Peace country, but his guide, Bocock, was the geologist in charge of the government's Resource Survey Department. The expedition made it to Dease Lake and, soon after, a pass through the Stikine Mountains was named after Charles Bedaux.

The 1934 journey was ostensibly a failure and both Godsell and Berton lavish prose on the mishaps of the vast, seemingly comical expedition. Ladies preparing their toilettes in the middle of the bush, Bedaux's wife handing out cigarettes to the wranglers, Bedaux's cameraman filming everything in sight, his funny tractors bogged down in the mud. But could Bedaux, the manager of men and machinery, have been so stupid or were the activities of his group an elaborate cover?

Bedaux was not inexperienced in the bush or in any other phase of getting along in the world. He had toiled years as a laborer and was a self-made millionaire; he was an experienced hunter, his trip from Mombassa on the Indian Ocean to Casablanca on the Atlantic covered ten thousand miles and he had made several mountain-climbing expeditions to the Himalayas. He could get along very well away from the Chrysler Building, the rue de Rivoli, or the Champs Élysées. He had already pushed through the dense northern bush as far as Dease Lake.

His 1934 expedition was not exactly a collection of nuts. It was backed by the Citroën Company and the British Columbia Department of Lands. The guide, Bocock, who had been with Bedaux in 1932, was the region's chief geologist. The government of British Columbia had donated two of its leading geographers, Ernest Lamarque and Frank Swannell. The cameraman was Floyd Crosby, who was the cinematographer on Robert Flaherty's great documentary films. The expedition was accompanied by local trappers, prospectors, and wranglers, all thoroughly familiar with the terrain.

Yet Berton writes that on October 22, Bedaux called a press conference to announce his expedition was over. He blamed bad weather and lack of feed for his horses. " 'But someday,' Bedaux prophesied, 'a highway will be built in the wake of the trail' that he had blazed."

Bedaux stayed in the bush while the others went back to Fort St. John. The reason was that he was waiting for Lamarque, who was in charge of the advance party. Lamarque made it to Telegraph Creek in the Yukon and reported back to his boss.

On October 26, Bedaux told the Peace River *Block News* that although the expedition had "failed" he believed he had "found the logical route for an international highway." No one, not even those who would write of his Canadian experiences, considered what interest Bedaux had in such a highway.

The next couple of years found him in India, Tibet, and Persia. He rented a home near Hitler's Berchtesgaden and renewed association with von Ribbentrop and Hjalmar Schacht and other German officials. In 1941 Bedaux devised a scheme for the protection of Germany's Persian Gulf oil refineries from Allied bombing.

In 1942 the Vichy government allowed him to organize the entire town of Roquefort in the weirdest social experiment since Brook Farm.

In the summer of 1943 he was engaged to build a pipeline across the Sahara to replenish the dwindling oil supplies of the Reich. Not only did Bedaux have Saharan experience but also he had built a pipeline before. Far away in the wilds of British Columbia. The impoverished town of Fort St. John was without a water supply and Bedaux had built it a pipeline from Charlie Lake to town through land with which he was supposedly unfamiliar. This explains his visit of 1929.

His headquarters during the Saharan pipeline operations was the Aletti Hotel in Algiers. It was there he was arrested on suspicion of being involved in Admiral Darlan's assassination in December 1942. Bedaux was released only to be arrested again by the Americans, this time on a charge of trading with the enemy. He was taken to Miami where, on Valentine's Day 1944, he died in custody in a room over a garage, supposedly of an overdose of barbiturates.

The records of the German War Department indicate that in the middle twenties, shortly before Charles Bedaux first appeared in British Columbia in 1926 on the first of five trips, a plan was devised whereby Germany hoped to obtain control of both North America and Russia with the use of a highway that would connect the mainland of Canada with the Bering Strait.

History meant nothing to her for she neither
spoke nor understood English let alone read it.

———

Obituary writer in Peace River
News on the death of Beaver Indian
Bella Yahey, at age 118

3

DAWSON CREEK ... It is a snowy afternoon in December and I am sitting in the Alaska Café downtown, such as it is, having a coffee and a piece of homemade mince pie and watching the passing scene out the big window decorated like postcards on a dressing table mirror with hanging potted ferns. I am also paying some attention to a couple of the other diners, but mostly I am ruminating on the passage of time. I am convinced that he who said the more things change the more they stay the same had Dawson Creek in mind.

"A lonely Godforsaken town" it was labeled by Froelich Raney, a *National Geographic* writer thirty-seven years ago. Today there are new, cheaply built modular homes tossed like a handful of dice, willy nilly, over the barrens, and a string of motels line the road in from the airport and the road out, Alaska Avenue, the Alcan. Other than these changes one realizes that if God has not forsaken Dawson Creek, He is not exactly wasting too much of His time worrying over the place. Isolated it may have been but, with its board sidewalks and wooden buildings, it was at least quaint—from this vantage point anyway—that day in 1942 when the historic troop train lumbered into the siding with a local man named Frank Lepine at the controls. Now it is a monument to the architecture of necessity catering to the oil men who move in and get out as soon as possible. But then it has always been so. In 1942 makeshift barracks, tent cities, and Quonset huts were set down around the few indigenous log cabins when the Army arrived and long, long before that some accommodation had to be jerry-rigged when the North West Company's tatterdemalion gang of trappers, factors, and ruffians came to the country.

Roderick Mackenzie, cousin of Alexander, probably set up a trading post right over there, down the street where the Hudson's Bay Company store is now and where inside there is a little Beaver Indian kid, great-great-great-great-grandson of the lady with whom Roderick dallied one lonely night, covered with beaver pelts in his lean-to downstream aways. And this little link in history is standing there next to the computer games counter playing video football, his parka is unzipped and on the front of his T-shirt is a greaser giving the thumbs-up sign, "The Fonz."

Just this morning I was talking to the town's hair stylist, a guy named Del, who had come up from Vancouver on a self-proclaimed mission to bring the tonsorial modem age to Dawson Creek. With gravity he had shared with me his beliefs: "Dawson Creek is ready for good hair care." But he had also lamented, given the fact that his Burnaby girlfriend had not been able to join him up here as of yet, "Most of the women in this town look like loggers."

Which is similar to what I am thinking as I look at the two women eating their soufflés in front of the window. They are each wearing bulky flannel shirts, baggy trousers, and yellow rubber work boots with green uppers. One of them has her shirt sleeves rolled to the elbows, revealing thermal forearms. Just then the one in the long johns puts down her cup and reaches under the table to caress the knee of her companion. The other smiles as the hand works its way along her cotton twill thigh and she reaches across the table to brush an imaginary strand of hair from her friend's forehead.

Framing them are the potted palms. Past their shoulders, an old Indian man and his wife are getting into their decrepit pick-up truck. The lady is wrinkled and wears a kerchief over her gray hair, and the man a cap with earmuffs. He stops to take a swipe with his leather mittens at the snow on the windshield.

Two years ago one would not have witnessed such a display of affection in the Alaska Café or anywhere else in public in Dawson Creek, but just last night on the television in the beer hall of the Windsor Hotel Archie and Edith had discovered that their niece was, well, one of those. Two years ago the Alaska Café was known as the Alaska *Deluxe Evolutionary* Café. It has since evolved though the ownership has remained the same.

It is run by a guy named Charles Lux and back then he proudly suffixed his name with the initials "B.A., LL.B." and printed his poems on the menu. One was his ode to his Christmas tree. It was a vegetarian joint back then, but now they serve chemical cream substitutes in those stupid little plastic pots and offer mixed drinks for $3.75. Charlie, alas, is a hippie no longer; in fact, he is running for alderman and one of the planks in his platform calls for better TV reception.

As I walk around the snow-laden streets of Dawson Creek I notice that no one pays me any undue attention. This is because it is winter and people assume that I must be working outside of town as a rigger or a Cat driver; otherwise, since everyone knows everyone else and knows I don't live in these parts, what would I be doing here?

I remember a trip I took up the highway one August with my friend Myfanwy Phillips to take pictures of the people and places along the road. Mif looked like neither a local nor a tourist and made no concessions to the dust and the rugged terrain. She wore the same high wedge heels, rings, and bracelets and eye shadow that she might in Toronto, New York, or London. Her idea of sojourning in the wilderness is to read the New York Sunday *Times* in a downtown parkette. She couldn't have aroused any more curiosity than if she was Melville's purple friend Queequeg praying to his little ebony idol in front of the Mile 0 sign in the middle of Main Street.

I remember we went into a restaurant for lunch one day and all eyes turned to gaze upon her. Two girls nearby shook their heads. One of them said to the other, "He's some guy from Whitehorse but I don't know *who* she's trying to be."

Surprising, this attitude in a town that has seen every conceivable kind of traveler. What did they think in the long ago when Twelve Foot Davis or big black Bango Mike came rolling into town to spend some of their Hudson Bay loot on libation? What about all the strange Army recruits from the cotton patches around Dyas, Arkansas, and the ghettos of Cleveland's Hough?

But most curious of all, a race unto themselves are the folks who ride into town from May till September in mobile homes and call themselves "RV people." A curious breed that has never had the Margaret Mead it begs. They roll into Dawson Creek, jump out of crazy vehicles called "Wanderer" or "Apache" or "Loner," and start snapping Instamatic pictures of the Mile o sign, and corner some old Indian to capture his image on a slide to project on the living room wall for neighbors in Dayton, Ohio, who'll be making the trip next year. They buy the *Milepost* at the drugstore, some more film, a box of Kleenex, a bag of potato chips, a bumper sticker that announces, albeit prematurely, WE DROVE THE ALCAN ... YES DAMMIT, BOTH WAYS, jump back into their Wanderer, Apache, Loner, and vanish down the road—only to be replaced in a minute by another one, over and over, all summer long.

Later this particular evening, I turn in to a hotel bar for a drink. The place sits along the railroad tracks and on the other side the Alberta Wheat Pool Elevator stands like a black skyscraper against the dark gray sky. In the early forties this stretch along the tracks was known as Scrounger's Row. Among the jumble of sidings, railroad buildings, and Army shacks were the offices of the construction companies. A scrounger was an employee of one of these companies and his job was to meet the incoming trains to hustle the best men and equipment for his boss. The old-timers knew a good scrounger could make or break an outfit.

I get a drink at the bar and nod to a guy a few seats down. He looks at me shyly a couple of times and I know he has something on his mind and wants to talk. He looks troubled but he won't speak immediately because of the local reserve. You can go into a bar in Dawson Creek and there'll be seven guys sitting in a room with nobody saying a word to each other until the first guy breaks the ice and then everyone starts jabbering away about everything they've been holding inside for the last hour. So it was with this man whose name is Clint. After the preliminaries he begins talking about his little homestead thirty miles downstream. He's dressed in olive-green workclothes and has a matching cap pulled down over his forehead. He has great black sweeping eyebrows that remind me of the elongated V's painters use to represent birds high in the sky over seascapes. The point of the V dips way down the bridge of his nose.

"I grew up on that land thereabouts. By Jesus, I sure don't want to see it disappear."

"What do you mean, disappear?"

"Just that, friend. They gonna put it all underwater with this here dam they're gonna put in."

"They're going to flood you out?"

"Sure thing. B.C. Hydro's gonna build their dam no matter what us people who lived here all our lives think about such a thing. Never mind we don't want it. Some big shots down there in Vancouver or Victoria want it and that's all that matters."

"How big a project's it going to be?"

"Gonna flood a million square acres is how big. We ought to put up some kinda protest."

Another fellow sitting nearby, an older man, says, "Not a thing anyone can do about it. They want it in, they're gonna put it in."

Clint ponders that a moment and continues, "Now I'm just a dumb farmer. Got twenty acres over there and drive a Cat in town to make it work, but what am I gonna have when they're finished? All I got is my land. Why, I grew up around those parts, they're putting it in forty miles downstream, and I know all that territory. Played on it as a boy, hunted on it, now I'm farming on it. As a boy I used to find arrowheads there and little hunks of pots and things..."

The Peace River country is native land, its past mysterious Indian history that was never written down and can only be imagined prior to the coming of the *voyageurs* and the traders. On my last trip to the Peace, Canada's oldest citizen, a Beaver woman named Bella Yahey had died in Dawson Creek at the age of 118. The obit. writer told some tales about her exploits with the bottle and the story was buried between the pipeline news and the weather reports from Mars. When she was born, the closest significant white settlement was at Fort Garry, Manitoba, 2,500 miles away.

At the time that France surrendered Canada to England in 1763 only the trading companies were interested in the great Northwest. In 1774 Joseph Frobisher explored a route that was to lead to the richest trading areas yet known and that later would point Alexander Mackenzie in the direction of the Pacific. He had left the Saskatchewan River and reached the divide between the Saskatchewan and Churchill River drainages. At the Churchill River, he met Chipewyan Indians and traded with them for fur. The Indians were headed for the Hudson Bay trading post at Fort Churchill to trade their furs, but Frobisher made them a better deal.

The next year Joseph Frobisher returned with his brother Thomas and an American named Alexander Henry. They continued west up the Churchill to Lac Ile-a-la-Crosse where they met Indians from Lake Athabasca who told them of the Peace River and a big salt lake that lay beyond. The Frobishers and Henry were thus presented with the due for the continental crossing but did not pursue it since their interest was in trading.

Two years later the North West Company sent a man named Peter Pond into the Far West. He followed the Frobishers' route and made it to the Athabasca River within fifty miles of Lake Athabasca. Here he built a trading post and remained for the winter.

In 1783 the Frobishers and Pond became partners of the North West Company, which was actually a loose federation of independent concerns. It soon became the largest commercial enterprise in North America. Pond meanwhile was organizing the Athabasca district and expanding it, building important forts on Slave Lake and the Peace River.

Although Pond had responsibilities for enlarging trade, he was a born explorer, venturing wherever possible into the surrounding unknown. He was a rough, illiterate, but inquisitive man and a man with a past. Born in Connecticut in 1740, he joined the army at age sixteen and served in the wars against the French. Later he was to pioneer trade with the Sioux. Pond had killed a man at Michilimackinac in a gun fight and in 1782 was involved in the death of a trader but was acquitted.

Pond wanted to know how to get to the Pacific. The need to reach the ocean was obvious to anyone interested in geography or involved in trade. The search for a passage from the Atlantic to the Pacific had been going on since 1535, when Jacques Cartier sailed up the St. Lawrence to Montreal. To the south, Captain John Smith, the founder of Jamestown, was going up every river in Virginia looking for the Pacific. In 1778 the British Admiralty sent Captain James Cook to find a passage. He failed, of course, but he did explore the Pacific Coast thoroughly enough to discover that an immensely rich trading business could be conducted with the Russians. The trade was also a great incentive to the Canadians, especially since British North America needed an outlet to the Pacific, which was nominally claimed at the time by Spain.

In 1788 a young man named Alexander Mackenzie was sent by the company to assist Pond at Athabasca. Mackenzie was born on the island of Lewis off Scotland and had been sent to New York State after the death of his mother when he was ten. As the Revolutionary War grew closer, Mackenzie was packed off to Montreal, where he entered the trading firm of Gregory and McLeod, which was affiliated with the North West Company. Mackenzie worked as a warehouse clerk in Montreal until 1784 when he was sent to Detroit to trade. Four years later after meeting Pond in Athabasca, Mackenzie wrote to his cousin Roderick, also employed by the company, that the older man "was tried for murder at Montreal and acquitted; nevertheless, his innocence was not so apparent as to extinguish the original suspicion."

Both men wanted to find the route to the Pacific. Pond had explored the area extensively and kept none of his knowledge from Mackenzie. Together they pored over Pond's maps and discussed the territory, wondered where the myriad rivers might lead. Pond was in a position now, with Mackenzie to watch over business matters, to continue his explorations. He had professed his desire to go down the Peace River. Mackenzie thought the Slave River might lead to the Pacific. Pond was right about the Peace leading through the Rockies to the Pacific, but for some unexplained reason he chose this time to return to Montreal, leaving the ambitious Mackenzie in charge of the Athabasca district. It was one of those baffling decisions that in the history of exploration can only be likened to Sir Richard Francis Burton's practically surrendering the discovery of the source of the Nile to John Hanning Speke sixty years later.

In 1789 Mackenzie went to look for the Pacific via a river that later would be named for him. The ocean he found at the end of the Mackenzie was the Arctic.

In 1790 he went to London, where he spent two years studying astronomy and learning to make observations in preparation for his next assault on the wilderness. He returned to the Athabasca region in October of 1792 and had his men build a fort on the Peace where it is joined by the Smoke River.

The following spring on the morning of May 9, 1793, Mackenzie set off into the unknown. With him was his adjutant Alexander McKay, two white men from his other journey, four *voyageurs*, two Indians in the capacity of hunters, and a dog. On June 9, Mackenzie met Indians who used tools made of iron that had come from the Pacific along the trade route he was looking for. Mackenzie continually encountered Indians who had never seen whites before. Indians who warned him to turn back. Who told him of huge monsters rampaging over the land into which he was venturing. They talked of men with wings who lived along the river. Men who killed with their eyes. Mackenzie pressed on and came to the forks of the Peace River.

During his winter at the Smoke River an old Indian had told Mackenzie that he would come to such a fork and had advised the explorer to turn up the river that came from the south. All the members of his party urged Mackenzie to ignore the Indian's suggestion and to follow the other branch, later known as the Finlay River. Mackenzie went up the Parsnip and on June 12 his party portaged "over a low ridge of land eight hundred and seventeen paces in length to another small lake." The lake held Pacific water. For the first time north of the lands that separate the Colorado and Rio Grande drainages, white men had crossed the Continental Divide.

A few days later he found a river that was to be named after its second discoverer, Simon Fraser. Despite the threat of mutiny and hostile Indians, Mackenzie kept on the Fraser, which in places is as treacherous as any river on the continent. During the second week of July he found the Bella Coola River and with a party of the Indians for whom the river is named set out to the sea. July 20: "at about eight A.M. we got out of the river which discharges itself by various channels into an arm of the sea.

The tide was out and had left a large space covered with seaweed." Mackenzie had succeeded. He had fulfilled a dream that had goaded men on for centuries.

During the years of trade development and exploration by the North West Company, a rival, the Hudson's Bay Company, had established itself in the territory. As the HBC enlarged its scope the inevitable conflicts arose. There were disputes over boundaries and fights between traders of the two companies. Both concerns operated under this tension for several decades until 1821, when they merged as the Hudson's Bay Company. The company held exclusive trade rights until 1869, when it relinquished its charter in their domain. Despite the trading activity the land remained unsettled throughout these years. Very few whites were attracted to the area because there was still so much of Canada that was not only unsettled but also unseen—a vast region that was easier to reach than the Far Northwest.

In the early 1860s the Cariboo gold-digging around Quesnel, British Columbia, petered out and the prospectors began to drift northward, first to strikes on the Omineca River and then the Peace. When the banks of these rivers ceased to offer their gold in significant abundance, many of the prospectors moved still farther north. But some stayed behind to become trappers and free traders, the first white settlers.

These were men like William Cust, who had been a 49er before hitting the Omineca and the Peace. He stayed and thrived with his own trading post at the upper end of the Peace River canyon. There was Harry Moberly, who told of his adventures in a book called *When Fur Was King*. Moberly lived as a trapper at the lake that now bears his name, but served on prairie surveying crews, and as a free trader and a Hudson's Bay Company factor.

The most famous of these men was Twelve Foot Davis. A veteran of the gold fields, he made a stake in Omineca. Davis had never been to school a day in his life but he was imbued with an innate business sense. He parlayed his stake into a chain of posts along the Peace River to facilitate freighting other people's goods outside to Quesnel. He is often mentioned in histories of the area for coming to the rescue of the early explorers. On his grave is inscribed:

† + †

PATHFINDER, PIONEER, MINER AND TRADER.

HE WAS EVERY MAN'S FRIEND AND

NEVER LOCKED HIS CABIN DOOR.

In 1875 the newly formed Dominion of Canada Parliament sent a survey party to the area. The geologists were headed by Dr. Alfred Selwyn. A botanist, Professor John Macoun, accompanied the party and both men published articles and left journals of their trip. They noted coal deposits, rock strata, soil, plant life, and temperatures. They were advised by one "nigger Dan Williams" of the wonderful agricultural possibilities of the valley. This was a chance meeting, for at the time Williams was in hiding from the NWMP. He was soon to be captured and hanged for murder in Fort St. John.

During this expedition and the later internal boundary survey of the forty-ninth parallel, Professor Macoun wrote that he admired Fort St. John and Fort Vermillion, and his descriptions of these settlements had the effect of encouraging a few more men to leave their homes in the East.

Meanwhile the Canadian Pacific Railway had sent a geologist by the name of George M. Dawson to make a survey of the area west of the Cariboo. He was to gather information on the physical features of the land, its possible economic importance, and other advantages for the passage of a railway line by the CPR. Dawson wrote glowingly of the rich soil along the Peace River Valley, of luxuriant growth even on silt. He told of grass as high as his horse's belly, of hillsides alive with goldenrod and Indian paintbrush, and of the shy native Indians. And a few more came to the Northwest. Dawson Creek and Dawson City in the Yukon are named after this diminutive hunchbacked explorer.

More came and stayed in the rush to the Klondike gold fields, but until 1899 settlement by whites was actually of questionable legality. It was still Indian territory until that year, when treaties were signed with all the Indian bands in the area. But it was a harsh land and it deterred most who attempted to settle. The first real influx of pioneers occurred in 1912 with the homesteading act, which parceled out land for a ten-dollar fee. So the Peace River Valley became a rich agricultural area with the town of Dawson Creek as its center.

Whereas Dawson Creek evolved peacefully enough, the history of its neighbor, Fort St. John, forty-five miles up the Alaska Highway, is steeped in violence, greed, and confusion. It is now a boom town lying in wait for the gas pipeline to come down from the North Slope via Fairbanks and along the Alcan. Cinder-block oil company offices, mobile modular construction headquarters, and Chinese restaurants seem to appear overnight. Workers blow into town to do their bit and get out, to be replaced immediately by another crew. The atmosphere of impermanence is the only link to the past.

In the old days if you lived in Fort St. John you never knew how long it was going to last. It has been moved, canceled, burned down, and rebuilt somewhere else. It had its origins in a settlement known as Rocky Mountain Fort. It was the first fur post in what was to become British Columbia and it was built in 1787 by John Finlay for the North West Company at the mouth of Tea Creek six miles west of the present town. A few years later it was decided to move the fort and it is here the confusion begins because historians are not sure where it was relocated. It was said to have existed fifteen miles from the current town at the mouth of the Pine River. It is the name Pine River that is the problem. In Finlay's day the river was called the Epinette. The river that now bears the name Pine, however, is a different one and it enters the Peace from the south just above the point where the Alcan crosses the Peace. This was known as the Squaw River in the late eighteenth century. Later these two rivers were named the North and South Pine. In the early 1900s the Epinette or North Pine had its name officially changed to the Beatton River in honor of Frank Beatton, the Hudson's Bay Company trader who was at Fort St. John at the beginning of the century. Whichever river Fort St. John was located on, the Squaw or the Epinette, it was moved in 1810 to the other side of the same river but still at the river mouth. It was run by a trader named Guy Hughes. The local Beaver Indians grew dependent on the fort for their livelihood and the company prospered also, trading with the Sikhanni Indians farther away. In 1823 the company decided to move their operation to Rocky Mountain Portage to be closer to the Sikhanni, who were the better hunters but who could not be supplied from the Rocky Mountain fort. This decision angered the Beavers, who viewed it as an insult at the benefit of their enemies. On moving day Hughes sent his men ahead with the canoes loaded with goods and supplies. He stayed behind to attend to the final details and await their return. While he was alone the Beavers killed him and the next day when his men returned they were ambushed and all murdered.

The company, fearing a full-fledged Indian war, closed all its forts in the area and that decision had the effect of starving to death a large portion of the Beavers whose dependence had been such that they could not return to the old ways of existence.

Fort St. John was not rebuilt until 1858. That was the year Bella Yahey was born. Who knows but that her father had been one of the Beaver warriors who killed Hughes and his men. She must certainly have known "nigger Dan Williams."

Whereas Charles Bedaux earned at least a few chapters in the history of Canada, Williams' past is veiled by stray illusions and titillating asides and buried in contradictory footnotes. But the clues to his real past are there, in old newspapers, RCMP records, HBC archives, and in the memories of some real old-timers. They lead one to another and his history may be revealed, however painstaking the search. It is worth it. There is no one else quite like him in Canadian history.

Macoun and Selwyn mention him in their journals; historians allude to his existence mainly as a troublesome local figure given to drink and claim-jumping. There are other mentions of Dan Williams that indicate he was a trapper, prospector, trader, and crack rifle shot. Crawford Killian, in his book on blacks in British

Columbia called *Go Do Some Great Thing*, writes that Dan Williams had prospected on the Omineca with another black named Henry McDame, and that Williams became the first settler at Fort St. John. Killian mentions that Williams was the first to grow wheat in the Peace River country. James G. MacGregor in his book *The Land of Twelve Foot Davis* recounts Williams' trial at Fort St. John, where he had been jailed for shooting at the HBC trader. One of Williams' buddies testified that the black man wasn't trying to harm the trader. Williams was such a good shot, his friend claimed, that if he wanted to hurt the trader he wouldn't have missed. "I know as many miners know that Dan at a hundred yards can take the eye out of a jackrabbit."

Thanks to this argument Williams' sentence was greatly reduced. After his release his remaining years seem lost in obscurity, with some commentators saying that he was killed by his prospecting partner on the Finlay River in 1887.

The only writer to mention Williams' origin is Killian, who writes that he was born in Ontario and came West as a cook with the Palliser Expedition. (Captain John Palliser, who led this expedition through the Canadian West in the 1800s, made the observation that the greatest single obstacle to the settling of the West was the absence of any road or trail through the territory.) He was, in fact, born a slave in the 1830s on a plantation in Prince George County, Virginia. He escaped to freedom by way of the Underground Railroad. Along the route his abolitionist helpers had preached the love of God and Williams crossed the Canadian border, his Bible under his arm. God on His throne had given him the Word and the Queen in England had given him his freedom. As an old trapper wrote about Williams: "He only recognized two masters—Queen Victoria and Jesus Christ! He was always writin' notes to one and prayin' to the other."

Williams worked on the boats around the Great Lakes before heading West perhaps, as Killian writes, with the Palliser Expedition. Justice W.F. Butler writing in the Hudson's Bay Company journal told of Williams: "...he came floating down the river; a solitary Negro-pioneer, cook, trapper, idler or squatter as chance suited him."

He did all these things and while he was doing them felt it necessary to convert whomever he encountered. He interpreted the Word literally and woe unto the man who differed with Dan Williams. One who did was a French trapper named Jacques Pardonet whom Williams, according to stories, was supposed to have killed in a fit of religious frenzy. Another account has him robbing the trading post at Fort St. John of several bolts of white cotton cloth to use in his baptismal ceremonies among the Beaver Indians.

After his release from jail for shooting at the trader, Arthur King, Williams vowed revenge. He killed an NWMP constable and took to the woods. He was befriended by the Beavers whom he earlier had given gifts in exchange for conversion rights.

One of the bands, led by Chief Komaxala, protected Williams and hid him when he returned from his sniper attacks on the company and the police. The chief also gave Dan his daughter in marriage. It was during this sojourn in the bush that he came upon Macoun and Selwyn. He was soon caught in an ambush, arrested, and taken once more to jail in Fort St. John. He was tried, sentenced, and transferred to Fort Saskatchewan where he was hanged March 15, 1878.

Bella Yahey was around at Fort St. John's beginning and she was a spry, young ninety-two when they began to build the Alcan. Around the Peace River country it is not difficult to find her relatives. There are dozens of them. One sat with me of an evening in the bar of the Windsor Hotel. He is a large, I mean, a *huge*, man named Freddie.

"Yeah," he says, his face grinning broadly, "the old lady was my great-aunt or something like that, I don't really understand."

He calls to the bartender, a fortyish blonde named Helen, for another drink and he tells her, "This fellow here he's diggin' up old bones. He wants to know about Bella!" They bring Freddie his rum and Cokes in oversized glasses. The ones we normal-sized people use would look silly in his massive hands. He wears brakeman's coveralls over brown workclothes and a brown cap pushed back on his round brown face that splits open frequently in a broken-tooth smile.

"Why, Bella the year before she died she was looking for one of us children in the beer parlor over there round the corner at the Alaska Hotel and she was there at closing time, you know loaded to the gunwales, and she couldn't find nobody to give her a ride home. They took her to jail and she spent the night. The Mounties they said they wouldn't give her a ride home because she smelled too bad. What they expect anyhows from an old Indian woman lives in the bush?" Freddie wants to play bullshit poker with Helen for his drink. They play a few rounds with him losing every one.

"Freddie, you'll play till you lose all your money."

"I know it. I know it. It don't matter. I'm just a big fat Indian."

They match coins a while and Helen gives up. Freddie turns to me: "She don't want me to get rowdy. I get rowdy sometimes." He breaks out in giggles. "Don't I, Helen?"

She rolls her eyes heavenward and says to me, "Twice a week I have to take him up to his room and put him to bed. He won't let none of the men do it. No way."

She gives a shake of her head and a look that indicates Freddie might get extremely violent, should that happen. I wouldn't want to be too close when he did. Close enough to watch maybe.

"When's the cabaret open?" Freddie shouts to no one in particular. He gets no answers from the tables but everyone turns to see whence comes the booming voice.

"Ten o'clock, Freddie, you have plenty of time."

"Thanks, Helen, I promise I won't get too rowdy."

To me he says, "They don't like me to go there because I get too rowdy. Everybody else just sits back, you know. Not me, I don't sit back."

He asks me whether I'm working in town and I tell him I'm investigating the Alaska Highway.

"I used to work on the highway when they was building it."

"Yes?"

"Sure thing. Well, I used to help my old man anyways 'cause I was just a kid. My dad he was a trapper and he used to go out in the bush with them Army fellows to figure out where they was going to put the road. Those Yanks didn't know where they were going till they got there."

As I stopped here and there along the Alcan, looked at the remnants of our old bridges, as I recalled the cold, the heat, the mosquitoes, and many other of the heartaches undergone while building our part of the 1400 miles of road in $5\frac{1}{2}$ months, I recalled the old saying we had in 1942—"The Road was built with Bulldozers and the guts of Men."

Colonel E.G. Paules, 18th Engineers

4

O N MARCH 26, 1942, two reconnaissance planes took off from Fort St. John with technical staff and special photography equipment to determine the best route for the highway. Shortly afterward an Army survey party left on dog teams to look over the ground conditions along that route. The teams were driven by experienced local woodsmen, one of whom was Freddie's old man. The push was on through the virgin wilderness.

The pioneer military construction of the Alaska Highway was divided into two sectors of operation. The Southern, from Dawson Creek to Watson Lake, was headquartered at Fort St. John with General James A. O'Connor in command and was comprised of the 35th, 340th, 341st, and 95th regiments. The Northern, Watson Lake to Fairbanks, included the 18th, 93rd, and 97th regiments and was headquartered at Whitehorse and commanded by General William M. Hoge. The 93rd, 95th, 97th, 340th and 341st were newly organized Engineer-General service regiments. The 18th and 35th were Regular Army combat regiments. All troops arrived with battle equipment, prepared to fight as well as build a road if the Japanese invaded the North.

The engineers hadn't known where they were going or what they were to do. In a report summarizing the activities of his company, "A," 18th Engineers, Staff Sergeant William T. Bennet, Jr., wrote that the men knew they were moving out and one of many rumors had the destination as Whitehorse, which was "known to be somewhere vaguely in western Canada."

It is perhaps difficult now to comprehend but the soldiers were constantly worried about the threat of combat. They had even moved out from their barracks in the lower forty-eight under arms with full field packs, helmets, and circles under the eyes. The men realized they were inadequately trained and Bennet remarks:

"We did not know whether the Japs had the strength to take the Alaska mainland, whether they might not come down the Yukon valleys someday and meet us in the forests.

"We had plenty of .30- and .50-caliber machine guns, half tracks and 37mm AT guns but we had never fired the .37s. Our first .50-caliber MGs were issued at Whitehorse but we had never fired these either."

Everything seemed so simple on paper. The advance crew at Dawson Creek was to lay railroad siding for freight cars so the cargo could be distributed. They were to erect the necessary offices, kitchens, repair shops, warehouses, and hospitals. Then the rations, supplies, and equipment were to be moved up the line to the camps.

Meanwhile surveyors and local woodsmen were to be blazing a trail through the forest. The "bruisers," bulldozers, were to come along rooting up stumps, pushing aside the muck and boulders, and grading the earth. The ditching machines would drain the road and civilian crews would then be ready to lay the gravel.

It happened that way, too, but a lot went on between the lines.

No one knew much about muskeg, moraine, permafrost, or glacial rivers. Supply turned out to be a nightmare. No one had considered workers might drown or freeze to death.

Plans called for the 35th Engineer Regiment to station itself at Fort Nelson, but first it had to cut its way there. It took them only twenty-six days to blaze a trail three hundred miles long. They crossed the eighteen-foot-wide Peace River by covering the ice with logs and sawdust.

It was the job of the 341st Regiment to build and improve the southern section of the road so that food and equipment could be moved up to the 35th. The May 21 edition of the Dawson Creek newspaper, which compared the Alaska Highway project to the Burma Road and the Panama Canal, also reported the worst accident yet to occur during construction. Men of the 35th had jerry-rigged a large raft to transport tractors to the head of the line on the far side of Charlie Lake. The soldiers were not prepared for the lake's sudden and violent winds. The awkward craft overturned and twelve men drowned in the freezing waters. Five survived only because a local trapper, Gus Hedlin, happened to peek out his cabin door as they capsized. He managed to pull each of the men from the water and drag them one after the other to his cabin.

Heavy equipment was used in three principal operations: clearing, cutting and filling, and grading.

Dozer operators cleared a seventy-five-foot corridor through the woods and bush. The D-C 8's moved in short sweeps lateral to the right-of-way, moving trees, boulders, and soil. In order to fell a tree an operator approached it in the lowest of the six gears and rested the raised blade firmly but without pressure against the trunk. Then he let the clutch out and opened the throttle all the way. He could not ease off until the tree was on the way down and meanwhile he had to be watching for backlash and falling branches.

After clearing, the cuts and fills were smoothed. The terrain was so rugged that a great deal of work with angle dozers was required. Wherever possible, cut and fill was done in the same maneuver.

Grading was the final performance. D-C 8's towed Adams graders. Because of the roar of the engines each man had to know his partner and be able to interpret his wishes through hand signals, which were apt to become rather original when made in concert with attempts to ward off mosquitoes and no-see-ums. This cooperation was particularly important because of the danger of hidden rocks in the soil. If the grader blade struck a submerged rock and the shear pin didn't break, the lighter machine would swerve and leave the ground, often injuring and in some instances killing the operator.

Most photographs of Alcan construction show the heavy equipment in operation and the majority of current magazine articles featured the work of these monster machines and their operators. Neglected are the pick-and-shovel men doing straight duty. Long days and weeks, tough, dirty labor, were put in by these duty soldiers constructing culverts and building small bridges necessary in the stream-riddled land to avoid drainage crises. Drift pins, spikes, and wire were the only hardware they used and the sole machinery was each company's one air compressor. The rest of the job was performed by shovel and ax, sweat and muscle.

Yet, still the building of culverts and bridges, the clearing, cutting, filling, and grading, were like puttering around the back garden when compared with the nightmare that was muskeg. The Army road-builders had never encountered muskeg or the permanently frozen ground that lay below. (Muskeg is bog or marshland composed of leaves and mosses and melted soil that has been rotting over the centuries.) Believing it impossible to lay a roadbed down over such a spongy mess, they stripped it away until permafrost was reached. On top of that they loaded tons of rock and gravel. But once the muskeg was removed, more subsoil melted and the result was a quagmire that had a way of gobbling up tractors, Cats, and trucks. The Army responded to the mess by heaping on more and more rock and gravel until eventually they realized that the rock and gravel had to be put down on top of the muskeg.

When first encountering the Alcan, the traveler might wonder whether the surveyors were drunk when they planned it, for it seems to meander where it might well have been arrow straight. A story has it that the road is so crooked because a Cat driver asked a surveyor where he should cut a path and the surveyor, looking off in the distance, said, "See the black object way over yonder? Well, keep that in sight and work toward it."

And so an oldtimer will tell you the road was built by following the path of a rutting moose.

Actually it wiggles and twists through the wilderness to avoid as much muskeg as possible. In the late summer it is quite beautiful, for the surface supports brilliantly colored flowers like yellow saxifrage, marsh marigolds, bog orchids, skunk cabbage, the poisonous wild calla lily, and fields of Alaska cotton. But you can't walk very far across the muskeg without sinking to your knees. So if walking on it is not particularly a pleasure, building a road across it must have been no fun at all.

When the swamp areas were particularly vast it was necessary to corduroy sections of the road. This meant that trees were cut down and the logs used as a track and support for gravel. Although corduroying occurred in places over the entire route, the biggest section was a fifty-mile stretch between the White and Donjek rivers in the Yukon. In some places five layers of trees and gravel had to be used before the ground could support a road.

Then there was the problem of drainage. As the permafrost began to thaw and flood the road, it was assumed that ditches would drain the water. But the ditches just kept filling and overflowing while water was also seeping under the road. The Army eventually had to fill the ditches back up and allow the land to drain naturally.

While the 341st and 95th regiments were working north from Dawson Creek, the 18th and 97th moved south from Alaska. They had corduroyed the fifty-mile section but muskeg, frustrating as it was, proved to be less of a problem than bridging the glacier rivers between Tok, Alaska, and Whitehorse. These streams changed their channels often and were ice-bottomed, which meant that bridges could not be built by driving piles. Everything on the Alcan was done by trial and error. Metal tools and equipment froze in winter temperatures that reached sixty below. The men would try heating them with torches or roaring fires, but in such cold the metal just shattered. They learned that equipment had to be kept warm all day and all night. Similarly it was learned that pilings had to be jetted. The hole for the piling was made by steam, the pile then greased, wrapped in tarpaper, and sunk in the hole. The hole was filled with water and the pile set solidly. The grease was to keep the piling from being forced out by the friction of the ice.

In the spring the soldiers had to keep twenty-four-hour guard on the temporary bridges. Ice jams rammed the pilings and had to be dynamited before they could crack and destroy the bridges.

Few of the soldiers had ever experienced extreme cold and most of them never dreamed such temperatures could even exist. Many were from the southern states and ill equipped to handle below-zero temperatures. There is the story of the soldier from the all-black 93rd Regiment. A local prospector came upon him standing guard at the Donjek bridge and said, "Well, how do you like the Yukon?"

From out of a mass of caps, scarves, and overcoats came his answer: "Yukon? Yukon have it!"

The cold brought tragedy. There were deaths from carelessness, but more frustrating were the many incidents when death could easily have been avoided. Men died from their lack of experience and their panic when confronted with the bitter cold. For instance, three soldiers were taking a truckload of used tires into Whitehorse. Their gas line froze four miles from town. They were discovered the next morning huddled together, frozen to death. There was an ax hanging on the side of the truck and the gas tank was nearly full. They had enough tires to burn for days.

Supply was a huge problem to the road-builders. Whitehorse was the Alaska Highway headquarters. After ships unloaded at Skagway, Alaska, material was shipped over the mountains to Whitehorse via the narrow-gauge White Pass and Yukon Railroad, which had been built during the Gold Rush. Dawson Creek, end of steel, was another supply point. In Alaska there was the territorial railroad and the Richardson Highway, which runs from the port of Valdez to Fairbanks. Aircraft, of course, were important. Planes operated among the points on the Northwest staging route: Edmonton, Dawson Creek, Fort Nelson, Watson Lake, Whitehorse, Fairbanks.

Meanwhile the U.S. Army had designed the Canol oil field project at Norman Wells on the Mackenzie River. It was built to serve installations and air bases along the Alcan and throughout Alaska in the event the Japanese cut off Pacific shipping bases. The Canol Road ran from Norman Wells to the Alcan at Johnsons Crossing in the Yukon. Thus, the great river discovered by Alexander Mackenzie served as a means of supply and support for the Alcan project.

Often ships and boats for transporting supplies to the ports at Skagway and Valdez were unavailable. Trains would arrive at Skagway from Whitehorse only to find no supplies waiting. In the spring of 1942 it was realized the highway could be completed on schedule only if the three-hundred-mile section from Whitehorse to the border could be finished by fall. If not, winter would cause a crucial eight-month delay.

The men in charge of this portion of the road, the 18th Engineer Combat Regiment from Vancouver Barracks, Washington, had to be kept continually supplied so that there would be no lost time. But mid-May found them still stranded in Whitehorse. Operations had been at a standstill since April. The supplies were not moving.

The men were as bored as the officers were frantic. The diary of one of the soldiers, Private First Class Robert L. Seaton, records the monotony of life in Whitehorse. He eats too much. Buys a .22 to amuse himself. Grows a beard for something to do and for something to do his sergeant orders him to shave it off. There are movies like *Tobacco Road* at "the local crackerbox." At night the men listen to the war news on the radio. "Bored . . . gabbed all night about agitators and skid bums."

General Hoge, in command of the Northern Sector at Whitehorse, was not bored; he was tearing his hair out in frustration. Where was his equipment? He traveled to Skagway and found a deserted waterfront. He flew to Seattle and found his bulldozers, his graders, and his trucks jamming the docks and cluttering surrounding streets because there were no ships to carry them to Skagway.

Hoge discussed his problem with E.W. Elliot, a Seattle construction man and Annapolis graduate. Elliot proposed to assemble his own fleet and get Hoge's supplies to Skagway. Thus was born "Elliot's Navy." He already operated a few tugs and barges through the coastal waterways and now began to add to his fleet. Elliot bought more tugs and barges as well as freighters, pleasure yachts, and even a schooner. One of his yachts was the *Sueja III*, flagship of the 1925 San Francisco Pacific All-Coast Regatta.

Before the end of May, Elliot had gotten most of the supplies to the 18th Engineer Regiment so they could move out of Whitehorse and on toward the Alaskan border behind the reconnaissance team. Besides trucks, bulldozers, and light equipment, the regiment now had twenty diesel "8" Cat angle dozers, ten diesel "4" Cat angle dozers, three half-yard Osgood and one 8th-yard Quickway gasoline shovels, three Galion road graders, and six Adams leaning wheel tow graders. A couple of months later, six monstrous Le Tourneau twenty-three-yard carryalls arrived but, as one soldier, Ralph Barton, later noted, "If they had come on time no one would have known how to operate them."

Fred Rust, regimental historian for the 18th, also focused on the inexperience of the men: "We were suddenly rich with a million dollars' worth of heavy equipment, brand new. To run it we had grocery clerks, fruit pickers, able seamen and cowpunchers, with a bespectacled school teacher thrown in."

It is the very fact that the Alaska Highway was built in nine months not by experienced engineers or seasoned construction crews but by grocery clerks and cowpunchers that ranks the project ahead of the Panama Canal as being the premier engineering feat of the century.

The reconnaissance team had left Whitehorse on the eighteenth of May and their experience is quite different from that of the other soldiers. The selections below from the team's diary might have been from an expedition of a century before.

> Friday 22 May… Road from Whitehorse to Kluane generally located OK except for minor relocations to avoid swamps. Stopped raining at noon, struck camp at 1:30 P.M. Saddled and packed by 3:50 P.M. Supper and to bed at 1 A.M. All tired out with sore tails. Pack train averages 3 miles per hour on road and 2 and a half on trails.

> Saturday 23 May… Pack train strayed away. Sent Johnnie Allen and Bobbie Cain our guides, after them. Finally found them 17 miles away headed for home. Instructed Indians to hobble horses in future. Jack Hayden showed us route to Slim's River crossing. Pack train rounded up by 7 P.M. Visited Jack Hayden that night. Typical old prospector and trapper. He is an American who has punched cattle in the states… Decided to get an early start next morning. Each of us saddled his own horse, then working in pairs saddled two pack horses and packed them. Indians throw diamond hitches when necessary.

Sunday 24 May . . . Breakfast at 6:30 A.M. Horses all saddled and
packed and left Kluane at 9:40 A.M. Jack Hayden guided us as far
as Slim's River crossing—there said goodbye and wished us luck.
Inspected bridge site, found no boat and water too deep to ford so
decided to continue up river and cross at foot of Kaskawulsh Glacier.
Found good campsite and fed the horses about four miles from foot of
glacier. Beautiful view of glacier from camp. Made camp at 5:30 P.M.
27 miles today. Saw 27 mountain sheep near headwaters of Slim's River.
Sent out a hunting party consisting of Major Mottern, Capt. Baker
and Bobbie Cain to restock our meat supply. Major Mottern bagged a
sheep and brought it back to camp. Marvelous scenery in Slim's River
Valley. Bear, moose and wolf tracks seen.

The 18th moved to the farthest outpost of the road-building job, in the Yukon near the Alaska border. Although supplies were now reaching Whitehorse, they were considerably thinned down by the time they reached the 18th. George Prechter was a supply sergeant with the 18th and he remembers, "The supply lines were so extended that for months the men were without adequate clothing and shoes, and food was at a premium. This was a result of supply convoys being 'robbed' by companies behind us. Our men lived on canned rations and often times men had to be taken off the work crews to put them on hunting details to shoot mountain goat and moose in order to have something to eat."

The men, it seemed, rarely got a full meal and when they did it tended to consist of the same old reliables. "Generally we had one fresh food meal a day," remembers Rust, "but we were on dry stores for a couple of weeks at a time. Powdered milk is powdered milk. The cooks made pork luncheon meat taste better by frying it in batter. They improved Vienna sausages by baking them in blankets of biscuit dough. But chili too is chili and no cook has ever been able to make the Army's meat and vegetable hash taste like anything better than silage. Fresh game furnished an occasional pleasant change, except for platoons 'A' and 'B,' which often had to hunt to live."

The company camps the men lived in were entire communities under canvas with an orderly room, kitchen, supply, PX, shower, laundry, and barber who, according to Rust, "was usually a farmer." The platoon camps, however, lacked everything but the kitchen and had to depend on infrequent visits of the PX man and the barber. The camps were hastily put together in or near woods and close to water.

"We struck camp, moved and pitched camp one day, were at work the next," the company historian remembers. "We built and bulldozed twenty-four hours a day, seven days a week. We lived dirty, we grew beards."

There with the "outpost" group at the farthest camp, Robert Seaton's diary had ceased being a litany of boredom.

> Arose at 6. Fried eggs for breakfast. Off to work with a faint heart at the prospect of corduroying a lot of road. Cut small trees all morning for the corduroy... roughride for chow. Rations lousy. Spent afternoon carrying and loading timber in trucks. Shoulder raw and sore... Good night, dammit.

In the camps it was all work. The only prepared entertainment was the occasional visit by the company band. Only one movie played the camps during the entire road-building project: Bing Crosby's *Birth of the Blues*. "Mail call," Rust remembers, "was the best phrase we ever heard."

But in the towns there was a different atmosphere.

From Mile 0 to the Richardson Highway at Buffalo Crossing (now Delta Junction), Alaska, the highway was pushing onward and the little towns that dotted the way throbbed with activity. The Peace River *Block News* of May 7 reported that in Dawson Creek "On Saturday night walking or standing space on the streets was at a premium owing to the large number of soldiers."

The soldiers danced with the available women, expressed curiosity over the Bennett Buggies—those horse-drawn automobiles left over from the Depression era of Prime Minister Bennett—and went to the movies to see *Pride and Prejudice*. That particular Saturday evening the first baseball game of the season was played, with Dawson Creek beating the United States Army Corps of Engineers, 9–2.

Whitehorse, a town of five hundred people a few months earlier, was now struggling to accommodate thirty thousand transients. The center of activity in town was the Whitehorse Inn, which ironically had been won along with three thousand dollars a decade earlier by T.C. Richards in a poker game with two Japanese businessmen. A New York *Times* reporter visiting the Whitehorse Inn described the lobby piled high with the luggage of strangers unable to get rooms. The beer hall was filled with soldiers, government officials, and construction workers trying to get a flight out. They all waited for the phone to ring and the announcement that planes were flying. When it did ring, everyone would pile into taxi cabs for the airport, only to find the flight had been canceled again by bad weather. This scene was repeated so many times that it came to be known as "baggage drill."

Soldiers walked the muddy or frozen streets. They bought hot dogs from sidewalk vendors. The steamboats carrying equipment left for Teslin Lake and Dawson City. Trains pulled in from Skagway. Planes landed with more and more workers.

Jukeboxes blared from log cabins that used to shelter sourdoughs. White women were a rarity. Indian women were off limits. The Army issued warnings: "The soldier has everything to lose and little to gain by indiscreet dallying with the native women."

One author, Gertrude Baskine, the first woman to receive a military permit to cover the Alaska Military Highway while it was still under construction, would excuse such dalliances by mentioning "...the days are so long and all the same, work isn't what the soldiers thought it would be."

Baskine herself was evidently in so much demand that she had to hide out a good part of the time in her room in the Whitehorse Inn. Later she recalled that time of enforced exile: "Eleven days I languished in Whitehorse—eleven endless, nerve-racking, frustrated days!"

All these men, so many of them raw recruits, inevitably drew the hustlers and sharpies from Outside. Soldiers with idle time and money in their pockets lost much of it to card sharps up from Seattle and off the Pacific Coast steamers. Truckers operated the most lucrative racket. After they delivered a load of goods they would have empty trucks on the return trip. Drivers quickly realized they could earn good money bringing out quitting workers and furloughed soldiers. Many of these men were so anxious to get out of the bush they would pay big money. The truckers charged whatever the traffic would bear.

The southern soldiers were particularly ripe to be conned. Some of their fellows did the conning. One author reports meeting "a bright coloured boy" with an unusually large roll of Canadian bills. He operated an exchange bank for white southern soldiers, many of whom regarded the Canadian currency as something a little less than legitimate and paid him two Canadian dollars for one American; this at a time when the Canadian dollar was worth more.

Then there was the good old boy who wrote home to Slidell, Louisiana: "You know, Momma; the British have got this country now but don't you worry, we'll get it back soon."

At the end of September 1942, Secretary of War Stimson announced the road would be ready by December. Canadian headlines proclaimed: YANKEES BEAT MUSKEG.

In the southern sector the 35th, 340th, and 95th regiments had come into Dawson Creek and worked north, meeting up with the southbound 341st at Lower Post, British Columbia.

To the north, the 93rd and 97th regiments, like the 18th, arrived in Whitehorse via the railroad from Skagway. From Whitehorse they moved to Watson Lake and worked south. The 93rd also built the Whitehorse-Carcross Road, which was so valuable as a feeder route to the Alcan.

The 97th had landed at Valdez, Alaska, and moved up the old Richardson Highway to Gulkana where they constructed that part of the Glenn Highway to Tanacross. Alaskan civilian contractors built the road from Delta Junction on the Richardson along the south bank of the Tanana to Tanacross and, of course, the Richardson Highway was already in existence to Fairbanks. The 97th bridged the Tanana River and opened the Alcan along the north bank to the border and on to Beaver Creek, where it met up with the 18th Engineers.

It was the 18th that had the roughest job. Their first piece of heavy equipment did not arrive until May 4 but as fast as it reached Whitehorse it was moved out. By June 15 the head of the regiment was near the Aishikhik River crossing and on July 1 the road head was at Kluane Lake. Here the various companies were ferried on Army Engineers pontoon equipment to points along the lake. The 1,195-foot pile bridge over the Slim's River was built from both ends with native timber and joined accurately in the middle. By August 1 the regiment was across the Duke and by the first of September, at the Donjek River.

Colonel E.G. Paules, commander of the 18th and after the first of October of the entire Northern Sector, remembers this final push of his regiment, the last phase of pioneer construction: "By October 1 we were working on the crossing of the four-mile-wide White River Valley. By this time it was getting cold at night and snow and frozen ground further hampered road work. Had all our heavy equipment been in Whitehorse by May 1st, this work beyond the White would possibly been finished by October 1st. However, in spite of the weather handicap the 18th reached Beaver Creek and joined up with the 97th in late October."

It was on October 20, 1942, that the Army work crews made contact twenty miles south of the Yukon-Alaska border. That afternoon Private Al Jalufka of Kennedy, Texas, working north and Corporal Refines Sims, Jr., of the all-black 97th and of Philadelphia, Pennsylvania, heard the roar of each other's bulldozers. They hurriedly crashed through the last remaining bit of bush to complete the pioneer route of the Alaska Military Highway. They touched the noses of their Cats and jumped down to jubilantly shake hands.

It is fitting that one was a white man from cowboy country and the other from a black urban ghetto. American history demanded it be so. Shirt sleeves rolled up, white hand and black hand clasped. It could have been Stepin Fetchit and Mickey Rooney.

John Wayne smiles. He's gotten the road through despite the skepticism of the pointy-head experts in Washington... Mickey throws his cap in the air with a "Whooppee!" Back in his tent tonight by the pot-bellied wood stove he will write a long enthusiastic letter back home to a small Indiana town of azalea bushes and white picket fences, a letter to Mom and Dad, and tell Judy and the gang that we made it and we'll win this darn old war, by gosh... Errol Flynn, upon hearing of the news, pauses for a melancholy leather-glove salute before hurrying on for his rendezvous with Olivia in a cabin near Snag Creek… Ernest Borgnine and the boys let up a big cheer back at the Quonset hut… They wake up Gabby Hayes around back of the bar and tell him the news: "This calls for a drink!"… But, at the Whitehorse Inn, where he has taken to snooping of late, Peter Lorre, from behind the potted palm, hears some soldiers say the road has gone through. He rolls his eyes and slaps his broad forehead… Back in the bush, Toshiro Mifune has gone into paroxysms of hysteria, muttering vile, hideous curses in that slope gibberish of his, before splitting back to Hirohito…

Dissolve to a montage of battle clips from the Pacific and European theaters and the narrator Lowell Thomas' voice mellifluously intoning, "Of course, the war was to last three more years. There were many battles to be fought on the land, in the air, and at sea. The toll in human life and suffering would be great, but it was this will to see men free as evinced in the building of the Alcan, a fortitude welded by the untamed wilderness, that insured the preservation of the democratic way. For it was here in the Northland, pushing an impossible highway through a primeval forest, that a fraternal spirit was forged such as would have made the war unnecessary had it been applied on a world scale."

Cut to the Stars and Stripes and the Union Jack crossed and rippling in the winds of freedom over a marvelous vista of the Alcan disappearing into the Canadian purple mountains' majesty on the horizon. The anthems of both countries blend as one.

The End.

There is no room in that little scenario for the fact that the first announcement of the completion of the road was made by Japanese radio. The U.S. Army made no report to its people for reasons of security. The bush might indeed harbor Toshiro Mifune spies. It was the same mentality that forbade the men to make reference to their work in letters home while at the same time American magazines were carrying feature articles on the Alcan by writers who had visited the road. Thus the soldiers clipped these and included them with their letters, only to have them extracted by the censors. The Japanese broadcast congratulated the U.S. Army on finishing the project and thanked them profusely, for it would greatly assist the Imperial Japanese Army in the coming invasion of the Western Hemisphere.

It was really only the beginning. The permanent all-weather all-year-round road still had to be built. The men were still on the job. On Monday, November 23, Robert Seaton recorded in his diary that it was "cold as an icebox."

> Rode out about 2½ miles and cleared PRA trail all morning. Busy, ate
> chow on the job. Exactly 7 months to the day after leaving the States

at 1 P.M. we saw the first 4-wheeled vehicle from the outfit ahead. Road now
tied in on all sectors. The vehicle (a jeep) contained a major from the 97th
and two civilian contractors.

On Friday he wrote:

Met and talked to some of the civilian construction gang that are
gravelling the road behind the 97th. All from Iowa... worked on snow
poles all afternoon and finished the job. Saw a couple of army cars and
one white woman (the first in 7 months).

Seaton and most of the other men kept working through the opening ceremonies,
which took place on November 20 at Soldiers Summit, a basalt cliff just north of
Slim's River and overlooking Kluane Lake and in the background the grand mountains of the St. Elias Range.

Colonel James A. O'Connor speaking for the Northwest Service Command and
the U.S. Army Engineers looked to the future: "The riches that have been opened
by the highway are beyond any man's imagination. The region opened by this road
abounds in strategic materials, in coal, water power and oil, and is suitable for
agriculture. For the first time means are at hand to tap this wealth. Its value will
outlast the war. Perhaps this highway, as a thoroughfare to Asia, and a conduit for the
riches of Alaska and the Yukon is destined to be one of the leading and significant
results of the war."

Peter Stursberg and Frank Willis broadcast the opening ceremony for the Canadian
Broadcasting Corporation from the back of an American Army truck.

The ends of a red, white, and blue ribbon were held by soldiers who worked on
the road. Representing the Northern Sector were Private Jalufka and another black,
Sergeant Major Sharp. From the southern end of the road were Master Sergeant
Andrew E. Doyle of Philadelphia and Corporal John T. Riley of Detroit. The ribbon
was cut by Cabinet Minister Ian Mackenzie standing in for Prime Minister King
and E.L. Bartlett, the Alaska secretary of state.

The bands did play "God Save the King" and "The Stars and Stripes Forever."

As soon as the ribbon was cut, the first vehicle gunned its motor and headed on
north. It was a battered weapons carrier driven by Corporal Otto Gronke of Chicago
and Private Bob Bowe of Minneapolis. They made it to the end of the Alcan late
the next evening, the first vehicle to travel from Mile 0 at Dawson Creek to Mile
1,523 at Fairbanks.

The 18th remained at work on the Alcan until the middle of January. It was a bitter winter. Before moving into barracks fabricated from green lumber at their own sawmill, the men of the 18th spent the month of December sleeping in tents. Seaton remembers nights when the temperature fell to seventy-two degrees below zero Fahrenheit. "All night we had fireguards walking around from tent to tent stoking our little Sibley stoves, keeping them cherry red while the water in our canteens froze solidly five feet from the stove."

For the men who built the highway, the time spent in the North was a valuable experience and they would look back upon this period in their lives with fondness. Some still meet every few years to swap yarns and trade photographs. Thirty-five years after his regiment left the Yukon for the Aleutians Bob Seaton revived for me some of his memories of this time:

"On our way from Seattle to Whitehorse we paid a visit to the Pullen House in Skagway and one evening after hours had a delightful conversation with Mrs. Pullen during which she described her eyewitness account of the shooting of Soapy Smith and the death of the vigilante, Reid, who plugged him. If I recall Mrs. Pullen's story, the vigilante's shooting iron misfired the first time, giving Soapy time to go into action. Both men lost their lives in the encounter.

"Whitehorse I remember as a friendly little town bounded on one side by the Lewes River and the railway, and wooded bluffs and an airport on the other side. Our camp was a ways beyond the airport, within hiking distance of town, a hike we dogfaces took at every opportunity.

"I remember the little movie house, Taylor and Drury's Trading Post, and the public library with the two cannons out front . . . One of my fondest memories of Whitehorse concerns a couple, Mr. and Mrs. D.A. Muirhead, who adopted several of us during our stay near town before we got going on carving a trail through the wilderness.

"Mr. Muirhead was assistant superintendent of the White Pass–Yukon Railway. Margaret, his wife, had a delightful English accent and several times they had us as guests at their summer log cabin on the Whitehorse Rapids. We had to actually drive along the railroad tracks to reach the cabin. The Army had taken over the railway and Mr. Muirhead used to joke that they broke all the records and schedules as well as broke up the railway. That train used to stop at Carcross and once while we were there killing time an Indian rushed out from the little nearby store and heaved a whole crate of apples into our car. We were a hungry bunch of 'doggies' by then and those apples were like the proverbial manna from heaven. And this when there was a war on and luxuries were hard to come by.

"Later I had the privilege of meeting a Mrs. Macintosh at her trading post in Champagne. I don't recall the exact circumstance but my buddy and I stopped our truck and went in the building half frozen, feet cold, and hungry. Besides some invaluable instructions on care of the feet and survival in the North country, she had a small supply of chocolate bars which she dug from under the counter to feed two thoroughly miserable soldiers. Bless her, too.

"After leaving Whitehorse our company [B] alternated with A Company in cutting the rough road, building conduits, corduroying, etc.

"I think we survived only because of the moose, mountain sheep and goats and the grouse, ducks and fish we were able to shoot and catch. Powdered milk and eggs, corned beef, Vienna sausages we were thoroughly sick of, as well as the three M's: mud, muskeg, and mosquitoes.

"Another unforgettable person was Leslie Cook, a bush pilot who kept us from starving many times by landing on scattered lakes along our proposed route and dumping supplies for us to work our way to. A side of fresh beef was a powerful incentive to build lots of road to get to such provender. Sometimes the ravens beat us to the beef and tunneled holes in it. We got what was left.

"Later we were all horrified and saddened to hear that Les had crashed his plane in front of the Whitehorse Library and was killed.... I still have the mental picture of his very pretty little wife in a plaid skirt pushing a baby carriage through the graveled streets of Whitehorse.

"I remember the cemetery with the little dollhouses in Whitehorse. Even more I remember a chaplain stamping into regimental headquarters one day when it was forty-eight degrees below and he was mad clean through because he had stood around for hours in Whitehorse waiting to conduct funeral services for a Sergeant Biles from D Company who had died of pneumonia. When the body didn't arrive, he checked around and finally located the body, which had been delivered to a ration dump.

"In addition to Sergeant Biles we lost one man to drowning in the rapids at Whitehorse. This was Lieutenant Small and we lost a crane operator named Morrison.

"There is one little incident I'd like to clear up since it concerned a friend of mine who just died a couple of years ago in the city of South San Francisco, where he was a well-known and successful doctor. This fellow's name was Salvatore Guardino and he was a major at the time. It is the incident of Captain Guardino's cat.

"Now all the outfits had pets. Dogs, cats; some had raccoons. Captain Guardino had a dog first, which he got soon after we reached Whitehorse. This dog was a little terrier called Sourdough. Sourdough would take up with anyone who was friendly to him, so Captain Guardino didn't have him very long. He got a little orange and white tomcat to replace him and he named it Shadrach. Now, each company in our regiment had an armored half-track vehicle equipped with a radio and .50-caliber machine gun. The radios were used to maintain contact between companies scattered along the Alcan. As was his wont, each night Captain Guardino would lock Shadrach the cat in the half-track of the company he was visiting to keep the cat safe from wolves, foxes, and lynx. Next morning the cat would be released to make his rounds and mooch from the mess tent. It fell to the lot of the half-track driver to clean up after the cat's incarceration. After a while the half-track became somewhat odoriferous, especially while parked in the sun on a ridge to better the radio transmission and reception.

"Finally one morning in A Company the captain released his cat, had breakfast, and set off down the road to his daily ministrations. It was at this time that the guys in the chow line noticed the half-track driver setting off into the woods, Shadrach by the scruff of the neck in one hand and a .22 rifle in the other. Shortly a muffled gunshot was heard and the half-track driver ambled back to camp with a satisfied smirk on his mug.

"For days after that the captain went from company to company running down rumors that Shadrach had been seen here or there and, as far as I was able to learn, no one ever told him of Shadrach's untimely demise.

"Well, I think because we built the section of highway the furthest in the boondocks, I think we had it a great deal rougher than most of the other outfits and we tied in the final link with the engineering outfit coming in from Alaska, the 97th, a black outfit. Some of us get together to talk about these old days but the ranks are thinning.

"Someday I still hope to drive the Alcan Highway and tow my trailer to Alaska. In the meantime I hope all the folks in Canada and Alaska will have a few kind thoughts of us instead of condemning us for opening the territory to overpopulation, smog, litterbugging, and all of the other civilized ills we are plagued with."

Gronke and Bowe had been able to drive all the way from Dawson Creek to Fairbanks because the road was snow-packed and frozen. The seventy-seven civilian construction companies waiting for their work to begin in the spring had little idea what was waiting for them. The muskeg and flooding rivers in the Northern Sector were so bad that the road remained dosed from Whitehorse to the border during the spring and summer of 1943. The Utah Construction Company had charge of this stretch north of the Donjek. Their work amounted to a massive job of draining and dumping. They improvised double-tread tractors that would push aside enough water so that dump trucks could hurriedly lay down gravel and rock from a fairly secure surface. Thus they inched along until October 13, 1943, when 283 miles north of Whitehorse units of the Utah Company working north and south met each other in their own private ceremony. Although unnoticed by the world, the Alcan Highway was for the first time passable all year round.

The period of American construction on the highway ended on October 31, 1943, and from then until six months after the war's end the U.S. Army Corps of Engineers kept up only simple maintenance. Commitment was greatly reduced.

The Allied position in the Pacific by now was stronger. The United States had reoccupied Amchitka in the Aleutians and were preparing to attack the Japanese at Kiska and Attu. The Japanese seemed to be concentrating their efforts in the South Pacific. The United States wished to transfer its forces to where they were needed more and there began the big pull-out from the North.

The Army left a road crew of only a few hundred. The Public Roads Administration moved its headquarters from Edmonton to Chicago and the ten thousand construction workers went home. There had been some tension between the Canadian and American workers over equipment and wages. If machinery broke down the Americans preferred to just leave it and go on. Many expensive Cats were rolled over in ditches and forgotten. This attitude was completely alien to the Canadians from the North country who were used to making do with what they had, holding things together with baling wire if necessary. The Americans seemed incredibly wasteful and they were, but it can be argued that there was no time to lose worrying over a machine when another one could be brought up the line.

Then there was the difference in wages. Americans were paid double or triple what Canadians made doing the same work for the same companies. But the discrepancy existed because of Dominion policies. The Canadian Government did not want its citizens spoiled by the inflated American wages. It was the same morality that drove the Canadian Government to change the name of the road from the Alcan to the Canadian Alaskan Military Highway due to the connotation, in the current vernacular, of the word "can."

During the first week of April 1946, the Royal Canadian Army took over management of the main stretch of the Alaska Highway from Dawson Creek to the U.S. border. The last of the soldiers moved out as the first travelers began to arrive. They had been inspired by magazine articles that hailed the Alcan project as a "miracle of engineering skill" and a "feat comparable to the construction of the Panama Canal."

But to anyone even superficially acquainted with the road-building job, any claims of miracles would have to be taken on faith. The Alcan, the winding road to the Far North, was constructed by prosaic old hard work and inspired by an old-fashioned patriotism that may never be evinced again.

1946: Go to Alaska by boat.

Business Week

1956: You'll be amazed how far you go to see so few people.

Better Homes and Gardens

1966: I remember sneaking a side-wise look at my wife during our first trip and noting with shock that the rich red color of her hair had faded and that her once-clear skin had the pallor of age. She is getting old, I thought, and reached over to squeeze her hand. Twenty miles farther on, when I took off my sunglasses to wipe off an eighth-inch layer of powdered road, I realized what happened: seeping silently through the locked car doors and tightly closed windows, the dust had not only aged us both but all but buried us.

Traveler in *Reader's Digest*

THE CHANGE-OVER FROM military road to peacetime highway did not occur until April 1, 1964. During those eighteen years the Canadian Government maintained strict control of travelers on the road. Permits were required until the sixties. Canada demanded a deposit or bond for all old vehicles or vehicles they deemed to be in poor condition. As late as 1960, drivers had to have a $250 minimum for themselves and their vehicle as well as $100 per passenger. The road was so rough that it was called a "junkyard for American cars."

In 1945 the Chicago Motor League reported that twenty-three million Americans were planning big postwar trips and that 20 per cent of them wanted to go up the Alaska Highway. They envisioned a tough trip through a rugged paradise. Imaginations were stirred by news service reports in local papers and the first magazine features.

Stuffy old *Business Week* was alone in discouraging such a journey. With them it became a kind of vendetta and for years every spring throughout the forties they published an article criticizing the Alcan and advising their readers not to journey North. In 1944 they claimed "tourists' prospects are slim."

The next year they warned that "tourists may travel hundreds of miles before reaching habitation ... Alaskan mosquitoes rank with the most vicious in the world."

And in 1946 they advised that "Alaska is not prepared for tourists," and anyway the trip would be boring because of the "unbroken monotony of thick forest." And not a broker for the entire 1,523 miles!

There were obviously plenty of folks who didn't read *Business Week*, for as soon as the war was over the travelers began to arrive in Dawson Creek. It was as if they had been crowding the old wooden console radio with ears cupped to the cloth speaker waiting for the war to end. As soon as Hiroshima was announced, they must have rushed out to the driveway and started packing. They set out in their prewar automobiles, tires piled high on the roofs, and water cans strapped to the running boards. Carloads of adventurers.

There was that great road up there waiting. Winding through Sergeant Preston land. There were grizzly bears and grisly prospectors, wild Indians, and Eskimos who rubbed noses and lived in igloos in Whitehorse. Who knows but one might park his '37 Nash by a pristine stream and while the fish were jumping out of the river and into the skillet, one might find gold nuggets at one's feet.

Imagine how these stories thrilled the blood of ex-GI's with postwar boom money burning holes in their pockets. They took off. A paperback novel by former traveler, John Olds, appeared, elucidating Alcan road kicks. The cover featured a beautiful dusky Indian maiden and a handsome rugged young gent eying each other in a log cabin motel room with a '47 Ford on the gravel road out the window. It was enough to make you get on that road and be gone.

And so they came, from Bangor, Maine, and San Diego, Tampa, and Fargo in anything that could motivate, Klondike-bound.

Magazines sent teams of people to cover the route as if it were a major expedition. And it was. In 1948 *Popular Mechanics* ran a three-month story, "We Drove to Alaska," that was typical of these articles. The authors encouraged one not to let "Caspar Milquetoasts talk you out of that long dreamed trip up the Alaska Highway."

The authors reported seeing few vehicles on their trip because although hundreds started out for the Alcan, many had to turn back because of mechanical trouble. During one 171-mile stretch they didn't encounter another car and over the whole trip they saw but thirty-five vehicles traveling in either direction. Many of the cars they did see were peculiar, like that of a twenty-year-old student named Henry Bucher. Henry was traveling from his home in Missouri to Alaska University in Fairbanks in a "decrepit 1923 Reo." He wore coveralls and drove barefoot. Henry had "converted his back seat into a bed and installed a small pantry and hot plate between the seats." He had cut the front fenders to accommodate modern-sized tires and had a washtub strapped to the roof.

In 1952 twenty-five-year-old Ronald C. Bulstrode bought a $100 used Cushman motor scooter at an Alaska Air Force base and drove the Alcan. He was written up in *Popular Science:* "When one man and his tiny vehicle challenged the world's toughest road, adventure hitchhiked a ride!" The writer emphasized the danger of such a trip, indicating that a scooter could not outdistance an angry bear.

The same year *Collier's Weekly* sent a writer, Leonard A. Stevens, up the Alcan with an independent trucker named Albert Hedra on "a journey few men would dare tackle." Stevens wrote, "More than once, my heart had been in my throat as we swept around a slick, steep curve ... of course there was the cold. Men have frozen to death driving this road."

But strictly speaking, none of these people were genuine tourists. Rather, they were officially approved travelers because they had each posted bond and been issued a government permit. The practice lasted for years. Writers in the early sixties would report seeing fifties-model cars being turned back as being too old.

Now, in the summertime on the Alaska Highway one views a seemingly endless stream of mobile homes, campers, and tourist cars moving through the dust bound for Fairbanks and coming back. There is still that lure of the unknown. Tourists write "Alaska or Bust" in the mud on their vehicles and many when they get to Fairbanks change that to "Alaska and Busted." The truckers call them "Pilgrims." But who,

I often wondered, was the first? That original authentic tourist? I pondered the question for years and endeavored to find out, *have* found out.

In 1948 the Canadian Government wondered whether relaxed regulations would not stimulate even more travelers to come North, and perhaps the money they left in settlements along the road might offset the government's staggering expense in rescuing them. It didn't work but from that month or so of relaxed restrictions one must look to find the original tourist. The absolute No. 1 among them. This was neither a mister and missus with the kids nor an ex-GI thrill-seeker. It was an Indian trapper from Teslin Lake, Yukon Territory. The reason he was the first tourist was because he was already there and he had a car. How he managed to have a car where there had been no road is a story in itself.

His name was George Johnson. Back in 1928 he had a particularly good trapping season and decided he would buy a car. He pondered over the make and model before settling on a new four-door Chevy sedan. When he announced his idea to the other members of the Teslin Lake Indian band they paid him little mind, suspecting he had, this year, perhaps stayed out on the trapline too long. As well they might, because a car was not exactly feasible in their locale, mainly because there were no roads. Nevertheless George sent his money to a Chevy dealer in Seattle who put a four-door sedan on the steamer to Skagway. The White Pass Railway sent George's car to Whitehorse and then via sternwheeler to Teslin Lake.

Now Teslin Lake is surrounded by thick forests and towering mountain peaks. When the boatmen asked George where in hell he wanted them to unload his car, George shrugged his shoulders and said the obvious: "One place is as good as another."

The fact that there was no road or even a trail upon which to enjoy his brand-new car worried George not a bit, for he immediately began to build one. Along with his nephew, he cut a path from where his car had been dumped to his cabin four miles away. For twenty years he drove his car up and down the four-mile trail and in the winters he would paint it white and take it out on the lake to use as a duck blind.

George had watched them build that road and wished he could venture out upon it. Then in 1948 when the restrictions were temporarily lifted, he got his chance. George Johnson gunned the motor of his rut- and stump-busted Chevy and wheeled out onto the Alaska Highway. The very first tourist. The entire Teslin Lake band had assembled and they cheered.

Indeed, one of the greatest pleasures of travelling was to find a genius hidden among the weeds and bushes, a treasure lost in broken tiles, a mass of gold buried in clay. . .

Basho, *Records of a Travel Worn Satchel*

6

S O I LEAVE Dawson Creek once again to travel up the Alcan, the bus nudging through streets laden with a record snowfall. After a mile of sprawl, neon drive-ins, auto-parts stores, new motels, we are in the bush, flat wooded land, the trees bare and their branches black and skeletal against the white fields.

Thirty-two miles along we cross the five-span cantilever bridge over the Peace and there again is the refinery and the pipeline that runs down to Oregon. Purple smoke puffs into the milky gray sky. I laugh to think of my journal notation of years ago. The one about the "indomitable will" it must take to live here on this desolate plain. I laugh because I had not yet met Jesse Starnes.

Jesse lives over there off the road in one of those trailers and he possesses exactly that sort of will. He is in his mid-eighties, but to him decades are meaningless notations, for he has the energy of active men a third of his age. His interests are boundless, his horizons limitless. He gets up every day full of enthusiasm and with a thousand things that must be done. There is his trapping, his gold-panning, his lapidary concerns, his study of astronomy; he has to tune his pick-up truck and take some geologists out in the bush and, hopefully, he can arrange an hour in the evening to read the old books about the pioneers. Mackenzie, Pond, and the greatest of all, David Thompson.

Jesse is their direct descendant. The lineage from the *voyageurs* and explorers traces smoothly to his trailer door. He came to Taylor when it was just a trading post on the Peace.

He was born in Texas and spent his earliest days there and in Oklahoma, which was then still Indian Territory. When he was still a boy his folks moved to a farm in Saskatchewan, but working a patch of prairie earth wasn't for Jesse. He took off for the West at the age of fourteen, just drifting. Stopping now and again to work as a logger, camp cook, or on the river boats. The work was just an excuse to allow him to wander around in the wilderness he so loved. He came to the Peace when he was seventeen and has been there ever since.

He built a cabin and set out a trapline, beginning in earnest to accumulate his vast store of knowledge of the natural world. Nearly seventy years later Jesse still says he learns something new every day. Walking through the bush with him one realizes that he reads the landscape the way other people read books. He seems constantly aware of the nuances of his surroundings, simultaneously noting the sunlight glinting off the poplar leaves, the smell of wild flowers, the wind rippling the river, the currents shifting, the myriad sounds of the forest.

I remember hiking in to the river with him one time. We had to cross a wheat field and he talked about that particular type of wheat and worried about the year's crop. We found a deer trail and he pointed out a raccoon spoor. We scared a covey of grouse from their resting place in the bottomland alder trees, and that inspired Jesse to tell me his favorite way of cooking them, which is to cover them with mud, unplucked of course, and bake them at the edge of a fire. When they are done the mud and the feathers come off like a shell, leaving the meat tender and succulent.

Jesse bent down to pick some rose hips and nibbled at the leaves surrounding the center and allowed as how he liked tea made from the flower. "If a man's desperate he can make him some tea out of spruce needles. It doesn't taste too wonderful but it's full of vitamins and it'll save your life. If those cheechakos'd known that during the Gold Rush they wouldn't have gotten scurvy. Grouse and rose hip tea has made me many a tasty meal. But, hell, a man don't have to go so far as spruce needles to survive. Believe it or not, them nettles over there make good eating if you dip them in boiling water. Anything that grows by water is generally good for eating. Like the lichen grows on rocks. Rock tripe I call it. Fish you can catch with your bare hands next to shore against the rocks. Good place to get them barehanded is by a beaver dam. Just muddy the water with your feet. The mud blinds the fish and you can reach down and grab them with your hands."

There is never a hint of the lecturer with Jesse; he doesn't come on like the self-appointed proprietor of the wild places. No, he is simply talking about what he loves and if he imparts information it is done incidentally.

The trail dipped through a thicket and we came to a five-foot-wide puddle which he jumped without a break in his stride or a quickening of his breath. He never missed a beat and kept on talking.

We came out onto a sandbar of the river and Jesse looked for the best place to do a little gold-panning and while he was making up his mind he casually mentioned he had just come back from Berlin, Germany, where he gave a gold-panning exhibit.

"Yeah, and I have to go all the way to Atlanta, Georgia, next week to give another one. When people started getting interested in gold again I reckon they got the idea of going and doing some panning. Somehow folks heard about me and started writing me letters to come and teach 'em. Particularly in Europe. So I got me a new career now that I'm pushing ninety."

Ninety, I repeat to myself. The word seems incongruous indeed. He bends down to examine the gravel. He's timeless as the river.

"I've always done a little panning whenever I had some spare time in the bush."

He still has the slightest trace of a Texas accent. His eyes are so heavily lidded he seems to be catching a quick nap while filling the pan. His hairline has crept back halfway on his scalp and patches of white and gray make wings on either side of his head and his nose is gently beaked so that he reminds me of a hawk.

"Never made much money at panning till the Depression. Furs weren't bringing in any money so me and a partner prospected for four or five years. Then it was back to being just a hobby until these last few years. Now I go to them exhibits and to contests they have. It brings me in enough money I can spend the summers traveling. I load up the camper and me and the wife head off to Alaska or Mexico. I do some panning wherever I go."

Jesse squatted at the edge of the sandbar, the blunt toes of his scuffed boots in the water. He shook the pan, tossing off the heavy rocks. A fish jumped in the middle of the river upstream and we looked toward it, a silver flash cracking the gray surface of the water. Jesse said, "I been trapping all along this river and I love it. It's the only river through the Rockies, you know. It got the name Peace because it's where the Beaver and Knistineaux Indians settled their disagreements. Indian name is Unchaga.

"I've always gone out in the bush with Indians. There's not many full-breed ones left. Never had any trouble with them, with getting along with them, but a lot of folks think they know all about Indians and know what's best for them. These people think they're experts 'cause they call them Native People."

I remember the line from the newspaper obituary on Bella Yahey, whom Starnes had known well, and I repeated it to him.

"Now isn't that ignorant," Jesse exclaimed, shaking his head. "Indians have very strong traditions and whites can't understand this because they think the only history and culture worth anything is their own."

We panned for an hour and came up with about twenty flakes of gold, which Jesse put in a half-filled medicine vial. Then we gathered up the pans and shovels and started back. As we were approaching the trail he bent down and picked up a couple of green and violet stones which I was about to walk upon. "Amethyst. I need them for some jewelry I'm making. I have a building out back of the trailer that I converted to a lapidary workshop."

We returned to Taylor and spent another hour in this workshop among the grinding, cutting, and polishing machines and display cases of stones and fossils. He had collected fossilized dinosaur teeth, insects, birds, and two halves of a dinosaur egg with the embryo clearly visible. He operates a mail-order lapidary business and maintains a voluminous correspondence with lapidaries as well as archaeologists all around the world. "Yeah, and I write to these fellows at the Museum of Natural History in Ottawa. Every once in a while some lapidary from Belgium or an archaeologist from Montana will knock on my door and we might have exchanged letters a few years back or he heard of me from somebody else, and we'll wind up going out in the bush for a few days."

We went back in the house and sat by the wood stove and he told stories of the bush, tales of wild animals and survival. Jesse's knowledge of the outdoors is pragmatic because for eight decades he has had to exist and earn a living from nature. Yet he is still filled with awe at the wilderness and maintains not superstitions, but rather an intuitive empathy with its mystery.

"One time I was at my camp and this female grizzly came into the clearing. She was hungry and started coming closer. I shot her. I was starting to skin her when I heard a crashing in the bush and her mate appeared and he was angry as hell. Now you can believe I was scared. He was only about forty yards away. I fired at point-blank range and I *missed* him. Now I *don't* miss. I fired again and missed again. He made a move and I started running. You better believe it. Then he stopped and went over to the dead bear and bent over her. Now I had as easy a target as could be and I fired. I missed and he didn't even pay me no mind. That grizzly started making the most amazing and scary noises I *ever* heard. He was crying, 's what he was doing. Sounded like a whimpering little baby. Now I figured that bear was gonna put two and two together and come after me, so I got my canoe and went out to the middle of the river. After a few hours he got up to leave and I took another shot at him 'cause I figured he might decide to come back. I missed again. After he'd gone I tested the sights on my rifle, checked it another time for good measure. Everything was lined up perfect. I set some targets a hundred yards off and hit them dead on. I can't explain it 'cept to say I just wasn't meant to kill that poor grieving grizzly."

Evening wore on and we sat there, him mostly talking and me mostly listening. He told his stories and discussed his plans, plans that would carry him through at least the next ten years. Eighty-five years old and in love with the world around him.

I got up to leave around midnight and he invited me back to go out in the woods for a week or so. As I was going out the door he said, "Say, thanks for coming to visit me. It's what keeps me young."

Somehow I thought it was more than visits that keep him young and this time passing through Taylor I had to laugh, like I say, because Jesse would never think it took any special kind of will to live where he does, but that was exactly what he has, all right. That indomitable will.

AS THE BUS MOVED ON through the snow north to Fort St. John my mind started wandering over other Alaska Highway experiences, people I'd met, scenes I'd observed, little tableaux of which I'd been a part. Other bus rides, car trips, truck trips, plane rides, walks, camping trips, hunting trips, and side trips. Some wonderful people and a few not so very nice ones. Everything occurring in the midst of this great land and with the road running through and connecting everything. The bus ran on and I was the only passenger save for a lone Indian huddled in his parka at the front of the bus, staring out the window with his own thoughts.

The streets of Fort St. John are filled in the afternoon. Pick-up trucks parking and unparking on the main street, sidewalks crowded with men stamping through the snow, faces hidden in parkas. The cafés are busy with workers on coffee breaks and men eating immense meals at two in the afternoon. Money is everywhere. New shops and stores, fancy restaurants. A man is in the *New Totem News* spending two hundred dollars on girlie magazines. He is in town from a bush camp to buy supplies. I walk around Fort St. John and away from the business district, the little homes are forlorn as ever in the snow, smoke billowing from chimneys as housewives make instant coffee and watch soap operas.

In the forties a writer noted that the Condill Hotel was the town's busiest spot as well as its most imposing structure. Now the letters of its sign droop and list and it is surpassed in grandeur by any number of new buildings. At night there are only a few Indians drinking inside. I recall another night in the Condill sitting with my lady friend Mif. We are minding our own business drinking a couple of Old Style beers and listening to Conway Twitty on the jukebox when a husky half-Indian woman in a nylon windbreaker, stretch pants, and cowboy boots approaches the table and invites herself to sit down. Her hair is combed the way Conway himself used to do his, back when he recorded "It's Only Make Believe." And she chews gum with her mouth open, lewdly, like a perverse southern sheriff. She talks out of the corner of her mouth, gives me a brother handshake but takes Mif's hand gently like she was a frail princess on a receiving line.

She focuses her attention on Mif, fixing her with a deep meaningful stare of Indian brown eyes. Every once in a while she shoots me a knowing look as if to say, "I know you're hip and we'll deal about this later."

At a table nearby a young Indian sleeps with his head in a puddle of beer. Over in the corner an elderly white man sits with his chin slumped on his chest, mouth open, saying nothing while his Indian lady companion curses him vehemently. I feel like I'm in the middle of a George Grosz cartoon transplanted to the Far North.

After the woman examines the rings on Mif's fingers with ever so much care and interest Mif begins to catch on. The woman must think I am some kind of pimp and I am considering my course of action should she get nasty. She goes at five-eleven, two hundred pounds, and looks like a half-breed George Chuvalo. She gets up and goes to the jukebox, puts on a Don Williams tune that was popular at the time called "(Turn Out the Lights and) Love Me Tonight."

The woman sits back down, waits till a certain lyric has played and says to Mif, "You know how we sing it up here?"

Without waiting for an answer and without taking her eyes off her, she sings it her way: "Turn out the light/spread your legs/and I'll love you tonight."

Is this for what Mickey Rooney built that highway out there? think I to myself.

Mif and I stand and get out of there despite the woman's most ardent protests and avowals that we can all be just friends.

But this wintry night everyone seems to be passing the old Condill by, trooping down the street to the Frontier Hotel and alone now I follow them. Open the doors to a sudden blast of noise, shouts, laughter, glasses hitting tabletops, and music from the jukebox. It is a low-ceilinged, brightly lit room wrapped in cigarette smoke. The drinkers are predominantly male workers in jeans and coveralls, many wearing those baseball caps bearing the company logo with adjustable plastic straps in back. Parkas are draped over chair backs or heaped on the floor and in corners. There are few Indian men, some Indian women with white men. Not very many couples. It is a masculine scene and any white woman venturing to the washroom is sent along her way accompanied by hoots, whistles, jeers, catcalls, and a stray grope or two should she venture too close to certain tables.

Soon the music stops and everybody quiets down for the main attraction. She enters the room from a door behind the bar and she is nothing if not statuesque, spilling out of her sheathlike gown; big dark eyes and perfect olive complexion. Now, despite all the beer-heavy, dirty clothes, rough talking, ready-fist activity, all that masculinity waiting to break loose, when she appears the men are models of decorum and respectability. Where a minute before they were ready to cop a feel from anyone's normally dressed wife they are silent and shy in the presence of painted fantasy.

She is standing to the side of the bar picking the tapes she will perform to and adjusting the machine. The men settle back, turn their chairs just so. One fellow gets off his bar stool and tries to engage her in conversation before she takes the stage. He reminds me of the song "Hello Country Bumpkin" ("how's the frost out on the pumpkin?"). If there were a Georgia woods nearby he would be from it. A long tall drink of water, is what he is, 6 feet, 4 inches and maybe 150 pounds if he had just been pulled out of the Peace. Dressed like the other men but with no seat in his pants. Gaunt face, shaved-up-the-sides hair. He ambles or rather sashays over to her side, drapes himself, all arms and elbows, over the bar and starts his patter. I'm too far away to hear. All the while she half-smiles, not looking at him, as she studies her tape collection. Then she excuses herself, cuts him, leaves him heaped along the bar with a whiff of Havoc.

The stage is in the middle of the floor and she hops up onto it and pauses motionlessly for a moment waiting for the tune to begin. Everyone is silent, she runs long cherry-red-nailed fingers through her wavy black hair and there are the faintest dark shadows under her arms. Then Waylon Jennings' voice fills the room and she starts to glide over the floor, slowly writhing, rolling her hips ever so gently and a shoulder strap drops as if by accident. The first number is just a warm-up, then, as "Bob Wills Is Still the King" plays, she begins to get down to it, grinding a little harder now, thrusting her pelvis with a purpose, bumping it to the bass line. Now she's strutting, tossing her behind with every short step and shedding her gown. You can see the sheen of sweat glistening on her chest in the bare bulb light. She rolls her rubbery, tassled breasts and offers her crouched back view over the edge of the stage. There is no teasing going on now, no intimations of the Kama Sutra, she is just working it back and forth lasciviously, bragging about her perfect body. All the men sit silently staring at her, transfixed. Hard laboring men with big arms, big bellies, swollen hands, and incongruous expressions, childlike, almost beatific.

In the middle of the third number she drops her flimsy G-string and there is a collective albeit faint catching of the breath. One man near me, middle-aged and hefty, watches it fall to the rough board floor. He stares at the G-string. What is he thinking as he looks at it there, so damned tiny and delicate?

One cowboy offers her his Stetson and she accepts it, covering herself with a fake demure fluttering of the eyelashes. She winks her triangle of glossy black hair at the audience and lies on her back fanning herself with the Stetson and wrenching her hips toward the ceiling and the heavens. Scissors her long chorus-girl perfect legs. The eyes ringing the stage miss nothing. Her body so near demanding rapt attention, its very presence excluding fantasies, occupying complete worlds now.

Then the final song ends and the magic goes with it. There is that horrible and ignoble moment when she has to squat to retrieve her clothes and walk through the crowd in her nakedness to reach the mean washroom where she changes. There is an embarrassed silent pause and then polite clapping. She nods in appreciation and then in a fit of inspiration, puts the Stetson over her breasts, pokes both inside, gives her chest a shake and prances away to sudden uproarious applause, saving the hour like a true trooper.

MOVING OUT OF FORT ST. JOHN, I sit in the back of the bus by myself. The only other passengers are an Indian woman who sleeps all the way to Fort Nelson and a mother and daughter who sit up front and talk to the driver. We pass Charlie Lake where the soldiers had drowned back in '42 and where Bedaux had begun his pipeline. It is a small summertime tourist site now, complete with a nine-hole golf course lost in the snowdrifts. Two miles farther on is the side road to the W.A.C. Bennett Dam, brother to the one that Clint had been lamenting back in Dawson Creek.

The pavement ends at Mile 94; not that it makes any difference in wintertime. The snow fills the ruts in the road, packing them and making the surface smooth and much more pleasant to drive on than in the summertime when gravel raps a steady tattoo against the underside of the vehicle and dust fills the inside. There are no tourists this time of the year when the traveling is the easiest and the country reveals itself as it is most of the year.

I remember all the other bus rides and talks with passengers who didn't have anything else to do but shoot the breeze and sleep, especially during the first three hundred miles to Fort Nelson when the scenery is flat and one vast stretch of lodge-pole pine and white spruce lining the road and far far beyond so that you could lose whole cities back in the bush and no one would be the wiser.

An ambulance sits in the snow in front of the lodge at Wonowon. The locals have been known to tell tourists that Wonowon is an old Indian word meaning Blueberry. Actually the post office used to be known as Blueberry but had to defer to another settlement of the same name down in the Kootenay region of British Columbia. Hard pressed to come up with another name for their one-building town, its few scattered inhabitants settled on Wonowon, which is another way of indicating that they are located at mile one-oh-one on the Alaska Highway.

I remembered the kid who got on at Wonowon one summer, seen off by all his friends. He looked like a chubby young Elvis Presley and he was wearing a gold and black satin western shirt. He told me he had to leave the area because his buddy had died the past week and it wasn't the same anymore in the Peace country. His friend, he said, had hung up his phone trying to use a 750 Honda like a scrambler. With no one to talk to now, I watched the snow fall outside the steamy windows and thought about some of those riders from past trips.

There was the young guy who had been working as a short-order cook in the Edmonton Holiday Inn and who quit to come North with his two Mennonite friends, who were sitting up front by the driver. When we got to Fort Nelson he asked me whether we were in the Yukon yet. When I told him no, he went back to sleep and I wondered why he had ever left his job.

I remember discussing the state of the world with Mr. Reis from Deptford, Saskatchewan, near the Cypress Hills where Sitting Bull and various outlaws used to hide out. Nattily turned out is the way to describe Mr. Reis. I noted that he wore flared cream yellow slacks and the white collar of his shirt folded over the lapels of his flashy sports jacket. He wore slippers but exchanged them for expensive leather boots whenever he ventured off the bus for a coffee. He would continually put on and take off his wide-rimmed sunglasses and occasionally his thumbs would lapse into twiddling. He looked like an aging, liver-spotted sharpy of the type that used to hang around the dog track in Miami Beach. He had, it turned out, been to Florida twice that year and had spent the entire month of January in Miami Beach. He told me he spent his time doing nothing but traveling, checking back at Deptford every few months to collect his mail. "I was in 120 major cities in America last year. I'm not a salesman either. Reason I travel is because I'm retired and I buy great big blocks of Greyhound and Trailways tickets at monthly or double monthly rates. I get in on all the specials."

He was going to Whitehorse and after a three-hour wait for the southbound bus was turning right around and coming back. "I'd continue on to Alaska but the special rate doesn't cover it."

There was the Swiss couple, newly married and on their round-the-world honeymoon tour. You knew this was their big fling and that when it was over they would stick close to home, become good solid Zürich citizens, never venturing farther than the surrounding ski slopes. Which in fact they verified. He said, "We want to get the travel out of our systems." They dressed identically in Adidas running shoes, strangely cut European jeans, and blue Nehru shirts. Whenever the bus stopped they would rush outside, both of them assiduously snapping pictures, arranging the passengers in groups, clicking at Alaska license plates, roadside signs, and tourist totem poles, all destined to be projected before their friends on an apartment wall back home, and perhaps I'll wander into a Swiss bank sometime to open an account—some hope—and the manager will think I look vaguely familiar. And well I should because every Christmastime when he goes to visit his friends, they show my face on the wall.

Click.

Lonely bus riders. Most travel alone because they are going on necessary errands, to visit relatives or go up the line to a waiting job. Only foreign tourists ride the buses. Others pile into cars or fly. Plenty of Japanese. French students amazed to see bears by the side of the road. Entire families of Indians.

We make the first stop this snowy day at Pink Mountain and after just enough time for some coffee and a homemade cinnamon bun start to leave. Another passenger gets on, a guy in his twenties named Dale who is going to Whitehorse to look for work. "Things got squirrely in St. John. Just Too Squirrely."

He says he does any kind of work at all. He's not too choosy. "Man's got to make a living."

As the driver is arranging himself in the seat a young woman runs up to the bus and knocks on the door. He lets her on and she shows her ticket. As she removes her parka Dale raises himself from his long-legged slouch and takes a look. Then he settles back down.

We talk about music. He says he likes country music.

"Me too," I reply.

He looks at me quizzically from under the rim of his pulled-down baseball cap like a sly old country fox. "I sure do like that Olivia Newton-John," he says.

"I thought you liked *country?*"

"Hah!" He slaps his knee. "I'se just testin' you."

We talk some more and then he yawns, gives a desultory glance out the window, and closes his eyes to sleep. I stare out at the forest broken only by creeks and rivers like the Sikhanni chief. The river is named after the Indians, the people of the rocks. Near where the road crosses the river the Sikhannis were victims of a massacre perpetrated by their old enemies the Beavers who for years had been seeking vengeance. The Sikhannis had always lorded it over the weaker Beavers, but the latter tribe being in closer proximity to the trading post at Fort St. John came into possession of rifles before the Sikhannis had ever seen them. The Beavers journeyed to the camp of the Sikhannis, vowing peace forever. After smoking the pipe the Beavers offered to display their detonating bows for the amusement of the Sikhanni children who gathered around. The Beavers calmly opened fire, decimating nearly the entire band.

A steep hill leads down to the river and this thirty-mile stretch to the other side of Trutch Mountain is the only variation to the flat monotony of the first three hundred miles of the Alcan. At the top of the hill overlooking the Sikhanni Valley Army workers erected a sign that warned SUICIDE HILL PREPARE TO MEET THY MAKER. It remained until tourists began traveling the Alcan in significant numbers.

I can remember one dusty gray afternoon a transport laboring up the hill with CIRCUS in red and orange over the cab and a center ring collage painted on the trailer with lions jumping through hoops, tigers growling in cages, a lady in a tutu on tiptoe on the bare back of a prancing palomino. I had just opened my eyes from drowsing and it was like a dream. I looked around the bus but no one else had seen the truck; they were all sleeping. Later we came upon the rest of the circus outfit camped by a creek; two more painted trucks, a camper, and a pick-up. A few men in cowboy hats and T-shirts stood in a circle smoking and contemplating the long jump to Seattle.

We pass Trutch, which was the first Army construction base north of Dawson Creek and the Prophet River. Trutch Valley was on the old Northwest Staging Route to the Aleutians and it became notorious as Uncle Sam's Million Dollar Valley because of the number of planes lost in the area. The Army claimed the accidents were attributable to murderously unpredictable air currents, but I have talked to local bush pilots who say the Army fliers were just inexperienced flying over mountainous terrain.

Fort Nelson was made by the highway. The original site, named, for some reason now lost in the mists of time, after the British admiral, is located ten miles away on the other side of the Nelson River. Until the Army arrived, the trapping settlement was accessible only by river or dog team. In the old days, by which I mean the early forties, the center of activity was Father Yvon Levaque's mission called Our Lady of the Snows. Father Levaque had previously to content himself with converting Indians and heathen trappers, but during the war he attached himself to the Army chaplains and had entire engineering units to help.

The town is a haphazard sprinkling of buildings clinging to its highway lifeline. The modular units and trailers now outnumber the log cabins. The Motor Hotel is the tallest building in town. A lot of money flows in and out of Fort Nelson and the people who keep it moving care little for the town's appearance. It is a winter town and now in December it is booming. Construction people, drillers, suppliers, oilmen are around jamming the hotels, bars, the Dixie Lee Fried Chicken store, and the airport.

The bus pulls off the road to the station, which is actually a sign in the window of a double-size trailer that functions mainly as a mail-order depot for construction machinery parts. The girl who got on the bus at the last minute in Wonowon disembarks here. She waves up the road to a pick-up truck coming to meet her. The man driving must be anxious to see her because he comes down the icy path a little too fast and his brakes don't hold. He rams into the front of the bus at two or three miles an hour, which necessitates a delay while we all fill out the appropriate forms claiming as per the driver's advice that we didn't see anything.

I go into the office and the floors wobble under me. The walls are thin veneer strips stapled to their joists. Sad to see. Transient architecture.

Finally we're off with a new young driver and they know this man, too, so the woman continues talking. They're moving in a couple of months to Kamloops. The driver knows the town well. His first wife was from Kamloops.

The road veers west and twenty-five miles past Fort Nelson begins the first grand country. The highway meanders through dense forest and then opens to incredible far-flung vistas, mountain ranges visible beyond wide river basins or vast plateaus of snow, all white plains save for strings of dark red water birch trees indicating the course of streams.

The undeniable beauty of the terrain was no consolation to the men putting the road through. After the section around the Donjek and White rivers this hundred-mile stretch out of Fort Nelson was the toughest part of the road to build. Mile after mile of corduroy was laid. So rough and winding is this section that it was intended only to be the tote road, but when appropriations were cut, after the engineers moved out, it had to suffice as the final route.

We passed Steamboat Mountain, so named by the Indians because the top reminded them of a steamboat, and ten miles farther, Indian Head Mountain, so named by whites because the top reminded them of the classic American-nickel-hawk-nosed redskin profile.

Then far down I see two wolves emerge from the woods to walk across the wide flood channel of the iced-over Tetsa River. Big white beautiful animals with thin, almost delicate-looking legs and heavily muscled shoulders. Their eyes are visible as pieces of pale blue glass in the all-white world.

It is dark as we pull into the Toad River Lodge. The lady and little girl get off here. An Indian is sitting at a table having coffee. "Hello, Eddie."

He greets her, "You been to the Big Smoke, eh?"

"Oh, yeah."

The Big Smoke being of course the site of the main campfire. In this case, the big town, Fort St. John.

Eddie has come to the lodge on his snowmobile.

"So you got it fixed, eh?" asks the man behind the counter.

"Yes and now I suppose I have to go back out on the trapline. I've had my three-week holiday."

Yes, Virginia, the times are changing. The cozy lodges are being modernized, replaced by modular units with veneer interiors and all the old team dogs hang around the trailer. Indians won't go out on the trapline without their motorized sleds. No matter that engine repairs can't be made at forty below and you can't eat a snowmobile if you get stranded. The old ways are dying out.

Muncho Lake. Years ago I had gotten off a bus at Summit Lake to bike the fifty miles to Muncho for no particular reason other than that all the flat land was left behind and this was the most rugged stretch of the northern Rockies. An area that abounds in moose and grizzly and sometimes you can see mountain sheep and goats crossing the road. I wanted to camp out at Muncho, "Big Deep Lake," and maybe do some fishing for grayling, Dolly Varden, and lake trout.

I hiked down to the shore and set up my orange nylon tent and gathered some small branches and twigs for a fire. As I did so I noticed a rowboat coming to shore. There was an Indian man and a boy in the boat. I went down to fill the pot with water and they came scraping up on the gravel fifty yards away. The kid saw to pulling the boat out of the water while the man gathered the string of fish and the gear. I went over to exchange a few words with them. They were Dogrib Indians, father and son. They had quite a catch, one lake trout must have been twenty-five pounds. The man had that smoky smell of a woods Indian. He was average height but round and solid. He wore a greasy sweat-stained hat and his hair was cut short. His kid was maybe thirteen and his chiseled features hadn't been blurred by age and weight. They had their pick-up truck at the lodge and were going home to cook the fish, but they allowed as how they wouldn't mind some coffee.

It was getting dark and there was a chill in the air. I got the fire started and it felt good. We all rubbed our hands together as if we were washing them over the fire. They were both shy. The kid said nothing at all and the father mumbled about fishing and the countryside hereabouts. It was all talk for the white man.

I made the coffee open-pot style with a little salt. The man said, "You know a good way to cut the grease off the top?"

"Eggshell?"

He laughed. "Yeah, that's right!" He looked at his son and grinned.

From a pocket of his red and black checked mackinaw the father took a paper bag wrapped in plastic which he unraveled and came up with a piece of dried moose meat. From another pocket he took a folding buck knife and cut off first a piece for me, then for his son and himself.

He dipped his chunk into the coffee and bit at it. Then he asked me, in a roundabout way, what I was doing up in this country. I told him I had come up to do just what I was doing now and I told him I liked talking to people who lived here and especially liked listening to their stories.

He took another bite of coffee-flavored moose meat and considered this and then he said, "I got a story I can tell you but it's a sad story. Wanna hear?"

"Sure."

To myself I thought I had never met an Indian who didn't have a sad story to tell. But he surprised me.

"Now this story happened a long long time ago..."

And I knew it was a legend he was going to tell.

"...and during the time there were only two people on the entire earth and naturally they were Indian people and they were from nearby."

"Naturally."

"Hah! Well, these two people were named Old Man and Old Woman and they were traveling over the countryside picking berries and catching fish and Old Woman said, 'Come on now, Old Man, we got to face the facts about what we're gonna do about people. It is time we put them on the earth.'

"'That's true, Old Woman,' said Old Man, 'but you got to remember I got the first say in everything.'

"'That's good. If I can have the second say.'

"Old Man he laughed and looked around him. 'Sure who else is there?'

"Old Man thought a moment and then he began his plans for the earth and the people. He said, 'It will be women's job to tan the hides. This they will do by rubbing animal brains on the hides to make them soft and then they will scrape them with scrapers. They will do this quickly 'cause it is not hard work.'

"'No, no,' said Old Woman. 'This I will not agree to. Tanning hides must be hard work so that we can see who the good workers are and they can be rewarded.'

"'Yes, yes. We will do it that way. The people they must have eyes and mouths and we will put them on top of their heads.'

"'No, no,' said Old Woman. 'This I will not agree to. We must put the eyes and mouths on the face so the people can see where they are going and can kiss each other without difficulty.'

"'Yes, yes. Well, we shall give people ten fingers on each hand and ...'

"'No, no. That is too many. I say, four fingers and a thumb on each hand ...'"

Now the father chuckled and said to me, "See, this is how men and women work. The man has first say but the woman decides everything. She lets him think he is boss. But that's not the whole story.

"So they went on walking over the land and deciding all these things and finally they had gotten everything taken care of except for the biggest question of all.

"'What shall we do about life and death?' Old Woman asked.

"They thought about this for a long time. They had come to Muncho Lake and Old Man said, 'I will throw this buffalo chip into the water. If it floats the people will die for seven days and then come to life again. If it sinks they will die for all time.'

"He threw the buffalo chip into the water and it floated.

"'No we will not decide that way,' said Old Woman. 'I will throw this rock into the water and if it floats the people will die for seven days. If it sinks they will die for all time.'

"Old Woman threw the rock into Big Deep Lake and it sank to the bottom.

"Old Man and Old Woman kept looking at the spot where the rock went into the water and they became sad that people should die for all time. Finally Old Woman said, 'It is better this way that people should die for all time for if they did not, they would not feel sorry for each other and there would be no sympathy in the world.'

"Old Man nodded his head slowly. 'Yes, let it be that way.' "They turned from the lake and walked away.

"After a year had passed Old Woman had a daughter but the daughter got sick and died. Old Woman was very sorry and she said, 'Let us make up our minds differently.'

"'No,' said Old Man. 'We cannot go back and change what we have agreed upon.'

"And so people have died for all time ever since."

IN THE MORNING I went up to the Muncho Lake Lodge on the highway for a big breakfast of hotcakes, bacon and eggs, and some strong hot coffee. At the lake, within sight of the lodge, a diving operation of some sort was going on. I watched the activity while I ate and the waitress told me a little girl who lived nearby had been missing and the other day they had started diving to see if she might have drowned. Yesterday a search party had found her unharmed wandering around in the woods. The divers, though, had come upon a truck at the bottom of the lake and the equipment was coming any minute now to dredge it out of the water.

I finished eating and watched the salvage operation. Along about noon they pulled from the water a tractor and flat-bed trailer with part of a load of steel intact. The skeleton of the driver was gripping the steering wheel. The license plates were Montana. The year, 1948.

Fireside. The lodge presents an ugly gray cinder-block face to the passing highway traffic but inside is a cozy sitting room with a fireplace and big windows overlooking the river valley. Adjacent is the dining room filled with truckers, their rigs parked out front, motors running. The boys are drinking coffee in thick mugs and engaging the plumply curvaceous waitress in some bantering of a mildly sexual nature. She coltishly tosses her blond locks, she's heard it all before, hears it every day, year round, keeps smiling, jokes back, and keeps them in line.

"Aw, when you gonna give me a chance, honey?" asks a Lyndon Transport driver going to Anchorage.

"What? You're always *working*, never here more'n a half-hour. I'm about convinced you don't ever have any fun."

"Hell, I can party like a *young* man," says the driver, a thick-set balding character in a faded blue cowboy shirt, silver belt buckle with a rig on it, and a big wallet sticking out of his back pocket and attached to a belt loop by a silver-plated chain.

"Now where do you figure we can party around here?" she asks, filling another driver's cup.

"There's always the back of my rig."

"But it's all filled up, ain't it, and you're going to Alaska."

"Yeah, well..."

Before he can think of another possible location, she gives him a wink and walks off, saying, "Look me up on the flip side when you're hauling air."

A little tableau stereotyped but true long before Bogart and Raft pulled up at all those diners in *They Drive by Night*.

On the wall down at the end of the counter is a display rack with copies of *Overdrive Magazine* and from the cover pouts the trucker's favorite fantasy girl, the No. 1 roadside attraction on the meandering route of dreams. And she's not a truck-stop waitress because a truck-stop waitress is either someone's sister or her old man runs the joint. She's, well, a pal. This cover girl though is something else again. The scantily clad phantom hitchhiker, the late-night, foggy-road possibility.

You've unloaded at Anchorage and are hi-ballin' for home having just popped a couple of potent biphetamine 20's, your eyes are bulging and the vein is standing out on your forehead and you're anxious to close the miles between you and the little woman back in Wenatchee. It's dark and lonely on the old Alcan, CB reception is bad this time of night, no one to talk with and John Austin Paycheck is conjuring up a lot of bad memories on the tape deck and, well, a fellow gets to thinking 'bout things. Wenatchee is only an hour and a half out of Seattle and the missus is only thirty-two after all and it is a Friday night. You remember that party, how she was necking with that dispatcher, a *dispatcher*, a couple of years back. You are away from home five days at a time and you don't hardly get a chance to get acquainted with anyone out on the road. But what about her?

Along the side of the highway the dark foreboding trees are closing in, as my buddy Dawson City poet Erling Friis-Baastad says, "like a bad marriage." Then up ahead at a clearing in the glow of lights from a motel on the other side of the road you make out a lone figure. A woman. In skirt and heels and peasant blouse, the top pulled two inches off the shoulder. The blouse Jane Russell wore in *Outlaws*, which you saw when you were a kid. The air brakes hiss and sigh as you downshift and ease up alongside of her. Broad face ringed with raven hair, big brown eyes and glistening painted mouth parted ever so suggestively, star points glittering off pearly teeth. There is a slightly evil sneer to her expression reminiscent of the girls drawn on the covers of all those old-fashioned pornographic novels that used to be sold at truck stops. She has sat on the edges of beds in motel rooms all over the country in stockings, panties, and bra, sipping rye neat from paper cups. Legs crossed, looking tough. She grabs her cardboard suitcase, lifts a foot to the high step and in doing so reveals more than a bit of thigh above the stocking tops. "Where you headed?"

"Seattle."

Johnny Paycheck is singing "I'm the Only Hell My Momma Ever Raised," and you think perhaps that is somehow not appropriate to the mood so you slide in Sammi Smith ("Take the Ribbon from My Hair for Tonight I Need a Friend"). As you ease the truck back onto the highway, she pulls out a cigarette and stains it fire-engine red with her lips and you catch her profile for a flash there in the dim light of the cab. The kind of girl who is used to earning her rides.

She turns to you, gives a knowing smile and says, "Light me up."

Idle dreamer, idle dreamer. Don't believe a word of it. Strictly negatory, ain't it? Come on?

Yeah, well. In actual fact, good buddy, what happened was I was rolling out of Whitehorse and there was this big old woman lugging a hunnert-pound knapsack and I felt kinda sorry for her standing out there in the cold. She was wearing overalls and a few flannel shirts and she generally looked like a big sack of laundry but then I ain't exactly no Burt Reynolds. Well, right off she didn't like my Haggard and asked me if I had any Fleetwood Mac and I thought she was talkin' 'bout some old Cadillac. Asked me my sign and I told her it was Straight Ahead. Damn if she didn't say hers was Yield. Then she rolled a joint and we got to toking up and before I knew it she was smiling at me a mouthful of big old yella teeth. Next thing I knew, good buddy, I was groping under all them flannel shirts and thermal underclothes. It was the weed that done it. Honest, good buddy. Ten-four.

THE FIRESIDE LODGE OVERLOOKS the Liard River. Liard, in French, indicates groves of poplar trees and the river is lined with white poplars. In the summer this stretch of the highway is bordered with yellow cinquefoil and blue lupine and it is not unusual to see a curious bear appear from the woods and stand waist-high in the wild flowers to peer at the passing traffic.

Just over Contact Creek at Mile 588 is the first Yukon marker and for the next 40 miles the road threads back and forth over the border. At Mile 620 is the Indian village of Lower Post, which was set up as a fur-trading post by one of the Yukon's first white settlers, Robert Sylvester, who arrived in the late 1860s. Later he sold the post to the Hudson's Bay Company.

It is here that the Dease River enters the Liard. The Dease formed part of the old fur-trade route to the Pacific Coast. Trappers followed it to Dease Lake, then took the Stikine to Telegraph Creek, where the sternwheelers departed, eventually going out to Fort Wrangell, Alaska, on the ocean.

The Yukon. Twenty thousand people in an area 2½ times the size of Texas. Fabled land. The first stop is Watson Lake with its rustic, wilderness village ambience lacking in the highway towns to the south. The highway parallels the lake, which serves as a float plane base. Both were named for a Yorkshireman who stopped off here in 1897 and said to hell with the Gold Rush. He married an Indian woman and stayed at the lake until he died in 1938.

Although Watson Lake is a busy little spot, a transportation and communication center as well as an outfitting point for hunters, trappers, and prospectors and the juncture of the Campbell Highway to Cannacks, Faro, and Ross River, it is probably most famous for the vast collection of signs posted at its northern end. Signs commemorating hometowns and giving the mileage to places like Palatka, Florida, and Avignon, France. Tourists gobble up postcards of the road signs and the guide books indicate the collection as a must-stop spot. In the summer one can hardly see the signs for the tourists snapping pictures of them. Thousands of postcards. Thousands of snapshots. A photo in every book on the Alcan. This veritable slum of signs is probably the most frequently reproduced symbol of the Highway, yet no book indicates which sign came first or who erected it. Just as there was an original tourist, there had to be an original sign. There is. And it wasn't easy to determine. One day Carl K. Lindley of D Company, 341st Engineers, stationed at Watson Lake, walked to the edge of town and for no particular reason other than a desire to symbolize his longing for the little town where he was raised, stuck the first sign in the ground and on it, in black paint, lettered: DANVILLE, ILLINOIS.

Just here over the border one becomes aware of the different breed of person who inhabits the Yukon. Although they come from everywhere in Canada and the United States and Europe, Yukoners are all different, all individuals; yet they are somehow stamped not only by the land but also by the spirit that has brought them here. The Yukoner is a more identifiable type than, say, an Alaskan, though this in no way diminishes his individuality. I noticed this peculiar fact on my very first trip and have wondered about it since. People come to the Yukon for other than the usual reasons that North Americans give to explain their mobility.

More than a job transfer or a desire to see something new. Why, this is one of the ends of the earth. Its northern border is the Arctic Ocean. Whitehorse is three thousand miles north of San Francisco. If you want to see something new you don't have to travel this far. No, whether a man is working heavy equipment or a woman is tending bar, they share that Yukon thing. Whether a person is a home-grown Yukoner or has come in from California he has got it. There is a romance involved and if people don't go around talking about it and examining it out loud that is no reason to think it doesn't exist. Some lined and wrinkled old fellow with his prospector's slouch hat pulled low over his eyes isn't about to wax eloquent on first meeting about the lure of the frozen North and the spell of the Midnight Sun, at least not until he's had a couple of drinks. Then, however, it will come. If you ask someone what it is exactly about the Yukon, he may look around at first and sigh, and knit his brow and finally begin, "Well..." Of course it is difficult to explain but you will eventually hear that there is a peculiar awe yet comfort in knowing one is surrounded by that awesome country and that just beyond most any mountain is land no one has ever seen; but there is more to it than the wilderness; there is that exhilarating yet melancholy pioneer feeling and the knowledge you are the last of a breed, one of only twenty thousand on hand at the end of a way of life, the end of the very last frontier.

Peter Mathiessen wrote, in regard to the Amazon, "The ends of the Earth have this strange allure that one is never asked about a past but can live day by day by day."

I have had the good fortune to visit the Amazon on a couple of occasions and I have marveled at its spooky green solitude, its jungle and river mysteries and been horrified at the encroachments of the modem world. There are parallels, yet the Amazon is a civilized place compared to the Yukon. The white city of Manaus had flourished and died before the first white man ever saw the Yukon. The river is the lifeline of the Amazon basin and I have hiked away from the river and into the jungle as I have walked far into the woods from the Yukon's Alaska Highway lifeline. There are more *things* to kill you, I suppose, hell, I *know*, in the jungle, but there is also the feeling that there is at least something in there. You cannot be, as the expression has it, one to one with nature in the Amazon. Not even if you are an Indian, I maintain. The Amazon tribes exist in an uneasy situation with the jungle. It provides and it kills. Nature provides the bounty and it oppresses and if the Sierra Club disagrees, well, then ask a Jivaro or a Machiguenga.

There is nothing oppressive about the Yukon wilderness. It is too awesome for that. Out in the mountains you are more alone than in the remotest corner of any Amazon. And it, too, can kill you. Survival? Think of it. What would be worse: lost in the jungle or lost in the high country at sixty below? In the jungle you might live forever. In the bush two days, three . . . a week maybe.

The first time the word "magnificent" was used, it was to describe a glacier in Kluane Park.

Before the grandeur that is the Yukon one can, finally, only be brought up full stop. Silent before the strange allure. . .

A FAMILY OF INDIANS troops through the snow from the Watson Lake Inn and gets on the bus. The mother and father are bent and stooped, wrinkled and slow; the four kids, all in their twenties, wear broad-brimmed hats and leather coats with long fringe. The bus pulls out and the mother opens a basket and passes around sandwiches and pours from a large steaming thermos of coffee.

On past the Upper Liard River, where there is probably the best example of western white spruce in the North; beautiful trees, some of them two hundred feet tall.

We stop for a break at Rancheria where I had gotten off the bus years ago and congratulated myself on finally reaching the Yukon. As if on cue, a Lyndon Transport truck pulls onto the lot just as it had back then. The driver gets down, a long lanky cowboy, and from the other side comes a woman. They walk hand in hand into the lodge, which has sadly been remodeled into inevitable modernity, which means

PHOTO GALLERY

OPENING PAGE: **Jim Christy by the Yukon River.** Photo Credit: Myfanwy Phillips, winter of 1976/77

PREVIOUS SPREAD: **First truck driving the ALCAN from Dawson Creek to Whitehouse, 1942.** Photo Credit: Anchorage Museum

ABOVE: **Soldiers on the Pioneer Bridge, 1943.** Photo Credit: University of Alaska Anchorage, Consortium Library Collections

OPPOSITE TOP: **Arrival of the first Greyhound bus at Jacquot's Post, Yukon Canada, 1942.** Photo Credit: Alaska State Library Historical Collections, Juneau

OPPOSITE BOTTOM: **Truck and soldier with duffel bags, 1943.** Photo Credit: Alaska State Library Historical Collections, Juneau

GENE JACQUOT GREETING MAJOR S. H. HOWE ON ARRIVAL OF FIRST GREYHOUND BUS AT JACQUOT'S POST. YUKON. CANADA

OPPOSITE TOP: **Bears along the ALCAN, 1943.**
Photo Credit: Library of University of Alaska Fairbanks

OPPOSITE BOTTOM: **95th Division**
ALCAN Highway, 1943. Jolly Johnson on
Trumpet Jitterbug Dancing. Photo Credit:
Alaska State Library Historical Collections, Juneau

ABOVE: **Clearing Land for the ALCAN**
Highway, 1942–1943. Photo Credit: Alaska State
Library Historical Collections, Juneau

ABOVE: **Edmonton (vicinity), Canada, 1942. Supplies for building the ALCAN Highway being transported by stern-wheeler.**

Photo Credit: Library of Congress, Prints & Photographs Division, FSA/OWI Collection

OPPOSITE TOP: **Army trucks along the ALCAN Highway form stiff competition for the local dogsled transportation.**

Photo Credit: Library of Congress, Prints & Photographs Division, FSA/OWI Collection

OPPOSITE BOTTOM: **Opening ceremonies of the ALCAN Highway at Soldiers' Summit, a stretch of highway 1500 feet above the wide swath of Kluane Lake, which is approximately 100 miles east of the Alaska-Yukon international boundary.**

Photo Credit: Library of Congress, Prints & Photographs Division, FSA/OWI Collection

OPPOSITE TOP: Meeting of 96th and 18th
Divisions, 1943. Photo Credit: Library of University
of Alaska Fairbanks

OPPOSITE BOTTOM: Frozen springs
along ALCAN 100 [mi], Nelson, 1943.
Photo Credit: Library of University of Alaska Fairbanks

ABOVE: Former lithographer Sherman
Gardner of Midvale, Utah, working as
surveyor. Photo Credit: Library of Congress,
Prints & Photographs Division, FSA/OWI Collection

ABOVE: Yukon, looking toward
Kluane National Park, 1976.

Photo Credit: Myfanwy Phillips

OPPOSITE TOP: Jesse Starnes, Peace River,
northern B.C., 1976. Photo Credit: Myfanwy Phillips

OPPOSITE BOTTOM: Alaska-Canada
border, near Haines, Alaska, 1976.

Photo Credit: Myfanwy Phillips

ABOVE: Dawson Creek, 1976.

Photo Credit: Myfanwy Phillips

BELOW: Red Feather, 1976.

Photo Credit: Myfanwy Phillips

ABOVE: Jim hitchhiking, Pink Mountain,
B.C., 2017. Photo Credit: Brad Benson

BELOW: Buffalo in the Yukon, 2017.
Photo Credit: Brad Benson

FOLLOWING PAGE: 72-year-old Christy
hitchhiking at Wonowon on the Alaska
Highway, August 2017. Photo Credit: Brad Benson

wallboard over old pine planks, a linoleum tile floor like in a trailer, and a plastic counter top, even a Mr. Coffee. The other truckers sit at their special place at the oilcloth-covered table near the warm stove in the kitchen. This trucker and his girl want to be alone. They sit on the chintzy side with me and an Indian man who is going to Whitehorse. We all drink coffee and shiver, keeping both hands around the cup.

In 1873 a couple of buddies were following the river looking for gold when they came to a little Indian village where the lodge is now. Being from the Mexican border area around San Diego, they gave the spot the name Rancheria.

NISUTLIN BAY IS AT MILE 803 and it is part of Teslin Lake. Teslin Lake formed part of the Stikine Trail used during the Gold Rush. Stampeders from Fort Wrangell followed the Stikine River to Telegraph Creek and packed overland 150 miles to the lake, where they built their boats and embarked for Dawson City. Many a friendship was terminated over the building of these boats. The most popular method was the "Armstrong Mill," whereby the log to be whipsawn was placed on a platform seven or eight feet off the ground. One man stood on top of the platform holding an end of the saw and the other man positioned himself underneath the log. The fellow on the bottom was the one who always got the sawdust in his eyes and down his neck.

A short way down a side road just the other side of the bridge is the little Indian village near where George Johnson, the first tourist, lived. There is an RCMP head-quarters there now, a seaplane base and a forestry building in front of which is a rock called Crow Rock. In the rock are the fossilized prints of crow feet and the Indians believe that if a white man puts his feet where the crow was, rain will surely fall.

Above Teslin Lake is a section of the highway built by the all-black Company L of the 95th Regiment and Brook's Brook is named after one of their lieutenants. Johnsons Crossing twenty miles from Teslin is the junction of the Canol Road.

The bridge at Johnsons Crossing is built noticeably higher than others along the route because the sternwheelers of the British Yukon Navigation Company used to pass underneath. During road construction the sternwheelers used to haul supplies to the Engineers working around Teslin. The sternwheelers operated from the Gold Rush era until 1955 when traffic on the highway increased enough to make them obsolete.

Locals call the little settlement J.C. The Indians insist it was named after George Johnson, who used to run a ferry service here after the highway was built, but the official view maintains that Johnson was a Canadian Army engineer who worked on the road.

Mile 865.4, Jakes Corner, was named after U.S. Army Officer Jacoby. It is the junction of the road to Carcross thirty-three miles away. This was the first connecting road to the Alcan from the White Pass Railway and it was used to carry equipment and supplies before the main road was completed. Along this Carcross road the American soldiers had put up a line of notices, reminiscent of the Burma Shave signs:

THIS ROAD... IS BUILT... TO SEND THE JAPS...
TO HELL... WHEN YOU... BUILD IT... BUILD IT WELL.

Just past the railroad crossing at Mile 909 is McCrae's Truck Stop and the alternate road into Whitehorse which goes past Schwatka Lake and the treacherous Miles Canyon, through which Jack London was supposed to have guided other men's boats to earn his stake in '98.

McCrae's was the jumping-off spot for a curious little journey of mine. I had been sitting in the Capital Lounge, "Where Miners Meet," a few miles away in downtown Whitehorse chatting up Marlene the bartender when a husky southern voice like Bourbon in old casks, like Jack Teagarden actually, inquired as to whether there was any action in town and if so where it might be occurring. The question was directed at me and I turned to face a gent with a ruined old movie-star face. It was as if the granite of his handsome sculpted face had begun to crumble. He had jet black eyebrows and jet black hair and I couldn't help but picture the little bottle of dye hidden under the cowboy shirts in his suitcase. He reminded me immediately of another gent with a husky voice I had met once who was, in fact, a ruined oldtime movie star: Lash Larue. His companion was a stocky blond, crew-cut kid in his early twenties, the man's exact opposite number, his son.

We discussed the activity thereabouts and he told me they were stopped for a little breather on their way to Fairbanks. "I'm Stan and this here's my boy Bobby. He's a B-52 pilot and he's on leave and I'm a country singer. From Tennessee originally. Gatlinburg. You know, like John R. Cash sings, 'It was Gatlinburg in mid-July I'd just hit town and my throat was dry.' "

He sang out and a few of the customers turned to look. He could sing too. When he noticed the folks staring at him, at his extroverted American behavior, he called to them, "My name is Sue, *how do you do?*"

They turned back to their drinks; a few even laughed.

Stan proceeded to tell me about his wife and Bobby's mother and how they had split up long ago and she hadn't let him see Bobby for years and now they were taking this great trip together to Fairbanks to meet up with the eldest son Lloyd who worked on the pipeline.

"Daddy, you don't have to tell everybody your business."

"Shut up, Bobby."

Stan kept emphasizing his position as a country singer and not only that; he had a little company back in Flint that published country music and recorded local talent. Stan said he was going to Fairbanks to sing in the bars and give those boys a little bit of home. Bobby indicated by various grimaces, head shakes, and asides that Daddy wasn't as successful and well known as he made out.

I led them to the Sandman Lounge where a rock band was playing and we drank some more and Stan by now was feeling pretty good. He began flirting with the ladies at the next table, paying no mind to the reality of their big, mean-looking husbands sitting there also. We managed to dampen Stan's ardor and turn his attention to the band. He immediately requested, in the middle of a number, that they stop playing that jungle music and do "Green Green Grass of Home." We in turn were requested by the management to leave.

I suggested we go out to the Copper King, a roadhouse on the Alaska Highway, but on the way out of town Stan saw the Yukon Inn and wanted to stop in the beer parlor. I tried to dissuade him. "It's not your kind of place, Stan."

"Hay-ul, boy, I get along with all kinds of people."

The beer parlor is the sort of establishment that manages to be well lighted and lugubrious at the same time. It is full of a type that is prevalent in the Yukon in the summertime. Arrogant, long-haired would-be sourdoughs. Guys who have recently arrived from Vancouver and pretend they've been in the Yukon all their lives. They used to make a daily circuit from the YMCA hostel to General Delivery to the Yukon Hotel. Some used to camp out on the escarpment separating the airport from the town. They would pitch tents of plastic sheeting and make fires. You would hike through there and find the wooded hill littered with cans and pop bottles and toilet paper. What they were doing was grooving with nature.

If you didn't look like one of them, and none of us did, particularly Bobby, your presence was not welcome in the beer parlor. Stan was rebuffed several times when he tried to start conversations. Finally he got the idea and we left. To me he said, "Well, I reckon there are some I don't get along with."

We went upstairs to the Quarterdeck Lounge and, lo and behold, there was a country band onstage featuring a lady singer with a swirling sculptured Loretta Lynn hair-do. Stan was home and fit to be tied. He stomped his feet and clapped and whistled. Against Bobby's imprecations he wrote a note inviting the band to invite him onstage to do a few numbers. Stan handed the note to the drummer who read it and relayed it to the singer who shrugged, why not.

"Ladies and gentlemen, we have a guest who's going to come up and do a few songs. Let's hear it for Stan, direct from Nashville, Tennessee."

Stan clambered up onstage, fastened himself into an electric guitar, and conferred with the band. He turned to his audience and started laying down a line of chatter. He thanked them, cracked some jokes, thanked them again, and offered bits of his personal history. Meanwhile the band looked at each other, the drummer did a few riffs on the snare. They finally got him to shut up and start singing, but he miscued the first time, coming in too late and inspiring a round of titters from the audience. Once he got going though he was fine and he sang that old prison tear jerker again and did "Is Anybody Going to San Antone?" He earned an enthusiastic round of applause and the band took a break.

Someone sent over some drinks and Stan was full of himself now. He recounted his triumph onstage and suddenly turned to me: "Boy, I'm gonna make a country singer out of you."

"You *must* be drunk, Stan."

"Nope, I'll teach you. Boy of mine here, he can't sing and don't like country music. Got him too much class for that. Likes Andy Williams or something."

"Shut up, Daddy."

"You come on to Fairbanks with us, Gee-um. I'll make a singer out of you."

"The idea is preposterous, Stan, mainly 'cause I can't carry a tune."

"I'll teach you the tricks. You got the right easy voice."

Out of the question, I told him, but he insisted I deliver a few bars of this and that, which I did, albeit a mite sheepishly. He said everything was okay and showed me a trick he did shifting the position of his Adam's apple to change the pitch of his voice. "Now you try it."

We continued like this over the course of a few more beers and Stan decided we should leave for Fairbanks right away. Tonight! Bobby cursed, argued, and groaned but what could he do? Stan was his daddy. Not only that, Stan also owned the transportation. They were staying out at McCrae's and the plan was to go back there, settle the bill, grab some Old Styles to go, and take off.

That was the plan but there were customers in McCrae's and Stan couldn't pass up an audience, especially if it was a captive one, even if it was comprised of only seven people. He went outside and returned with his Martin guitar with fancy woven strap. He commandeered a chair, tuned up, and began his patter, mentioning he was a genuine personal friend of Mr. John R. Cash. "Nobody knows him calls him Johnny, most just call him sir, but generally you don't speak unless spoken to."

Bobby tried to get Stan to leave but he wasn't having any of it. Bobby told him we'd be back for him in an hour and he better be ready to go then. Bobby told the bartender that he was not under any condition to serve his father any more booze.

Bobby and I drove down to the Copper King and caught a set. Or at least I did.

Bobby cursed out his father and told me his version of their entire screwed-up life. By the time we left to go back Bobby was drunk himself. He nodded off in the car.

I was surprised to see Stan sitting in the driver's seat of the pick-up sipping at a thermos of coffee. "Ah'm invested with amazing powers of recuperation."

We dragged Bobby into the truck and took off for Alaska. When he saw that his son was indeed sound asleep, Stan rolled down the window and tossed out his coffee. "That was for his benefit." He plucked a couple of Old Styles from under the seat, handed me one and said, "Let's us haul ass."

So we took off down the Alaska Highway, guzzling beer and singing whatever we could remember of C&W hits of yesterday. An hour into the trip I had begun to consider that this little venture was entirely feasible, that somehow upon landing in Fairbanks I would find myself transformed into a bona fide country troubadour. Two hours into the trip, I was asleep.

Sometime later I was shaken awake. My eyes felt as if they were covered with battery acid. My mouth felt like I had spent the night licking J.B. Stetson hats. Stan was grinning and blowing foul-awful breath my way. "Wake up, we're in Alaska!"

"Huh, what? Already?"

"Yep, look here at the water over yonder. We're at a little town."

"Water? What do you mean, water?"

"Come out, looky see."

I didn't have to look but I did. I knew where we were. There was indeed a town and water.

"The road ends here and ..."

"Yeah, Stan. You bet it does."

"Guess we got to wait for the ferry to get to the other side. This here is Haines, Alaska."

"Yeah, I know and you know what the place on the other side of the Sound is called?"

"Nope. What's its name?"

"Japan."

"Huh?"

Stan had missed the turn back at Haines Junction where the Alaska Highway bears right. There are a couple of signs warning you not to go straight if you want to stay on the Alcan.

"Damn," he muttered to himself. He looked like a guilty dog who had just chewed the slippers. "She-et. Don't wake Bobby. We'll just get in the truck and go back there to the turn-off."

We started walking back to the truck and Stan stopped cold in his tracks, stared back at the way we'd just come, and closed his eyes. "Oh, good holy Jesus!"

"What's the matter?"

"Oh, sweet muttering baby Jesus. Bobby's gonna kick my ass good. Oh, what am I gonna do?"

"What happened?"

"Forgot the trailer."

"What?"

"Airstream. Plumb forgot it."

So we got in the truck and headed back to Whitehorse. Bobby woke up in half an hour and when he realized the situation he cursed his father regally. Cursed him for every kid who ever wanted to bad-mouth his old man. Cursed him the entire two hours and thirty minutes back to McCrae's. Stan never uttered a sound. Nobody said a word to me. My hopes of country-singing stardom, dashed.

PAST THE AIRPORT AND DOWN Two Mile Hill to Whitehorse where the town is just waking up in the dead black morning. The first cars are creeping along in the snowy world, exhaust hanging in the air in dense clouds. The Indian family had gotten off the bus near Teslin, leaving myself and the Indian man I had been talking to at Rancheria as the lone passengers. There is a white man in the dingy bus station waiting room and he approaches the Indian. "Are you George Niash?"

The Indian nods.

"I'm from the company. I came to give you a ride to camp."

George doesn't reply. He sits down on a plastic chair, stares straight ahead. The white man says, "You coming?"

No answer.

The white man looks at him. Stands uncomfortably for a few minutes shifting his weight from foot to foot. "Don't you want your job?"

No answer. George stares across the room at the hound painted on the wall.

The white man looks at me, shakes his head in unsurprised disgust, and walks out.

When he's gone George smiles at me. "Well, I got me a free ride to the Big Smoke."

I grab my duffel and go out into the cold. Walking down Second Avenue in the bleak dark morning I can make out the signs of progress. A new RCMP headquarters, new bars. Ah, Whitehorse. More alcoholic beverage consumed here per capita than any other town or city in the world. I see the Whitehorse *Star* has vending machines on the street and, lo and behold, it is now a daily, save weekends.

When I get to Main Street I notice that the Whitehorse Inn is closed down and boarded up. It is to be replaced by a modern bank. It should be preserved as a historical monument. What will the city be without the tall prancing white stallion hanging over the sidewalk? It was the hottest scene in town during the war and the roughest afterward. It became the main Indian drinking and brawling spot, earning the nickname Moccasin Square Garden. Next door, John the barber is just turning on his lights, removing his parka to reveal a thermal undershirt. He takes his gold-colored nylon shirt off a silver hook and puts it on. A truck has been parked out front and the driver gets out and enters the shop. John whisks a chair clean with his cloth and extends a hand.

I cross the street to the Edgewater Hotel and go into the lobby. The little lady behind the counter smiles. "I've been wondering what happened to you. You have some mail."

Mail! After signing the register and catching up on old times I take the two pieces of mail into the coffee shop and order breakfast. One envelope contains my Yukon driver's license. The other, nearly two years old, informs me that my application for a job on the Arctic Circle as a weather technician for the winter of '77–'78 has been turned down.

As I'm sipping my coffee a middle-aged woman who looks familiar enters the café. I can't place her at first but then she sees me, comes over, and says, "Why, that turned out to be a real good car you sold me."

Then I remembered her. I had gotten the car in Whitehorse, used it to go to Alaska that last trip, and sold it to the lady when I left to go Outside. Two years later she was still driving the old car.

Mif and I had found it, a '67 Chevy, in back of a garage on Fourth Avenue. We bought it to take to the highway to Fairbanks. As I sat there eating breakfast I remembered that trip.

... Alaska is the last place for people like me.
The lower forty-eight, it's all crowded and crazy....
World's changing, son, and what I'm doing
is running away from it.

A traveler from Arkansas

W E DROVE OUT of Whitehorse through the old copper mining country northwest of town. The mountains there are rounded and gray and they watched over their wooded plains and late August meadows alive with delicate blue Jacob's-ladder with little yellow eyes in the flower and, of course, the pink and yellow fireweed which the Indians call the consolation flower because it appears after a forest fire and remains in old burns. It was this same flower that grew in London among the rubble of bombed buildings.

On to Haines Junction, nestled below the towering peaks of the St. Elias Range. They stand in iron-gray majesty above the little town and the icy trails through the passes mark the path of moist Pacific air like fingers of melted white candle wax. We stop at Mother's Cozy Corner set in the mountain shadows.

SMALL IN SIZE

BUT

BIG IN HOSPITALITY

We order pie and coffee and in comes an elderly couple, from Texas according to the plates on their camper. She is a buxom, graying nonstop monologuist and her husband bears an expression of resigned irritation. She comes through the screen door like a television announcer: "Oh my, what a cute little place. There are pies on the counter and they look so fresh. Hmm, now I wonder if we can get a glass of water here. I could really go for a glass of water and I am hungry. I haven't had anything to eat since that town a while back, what was it? Whitehorse, yes. Of course, I *could* just have an itsy-bitsy piece of pie and wait till we get to Alaska. Are there any Cheezies in the car, dear? No, never mind. I'll have a meal. Where's the waiter, where's the menu? Oh, look at the cute little signs on the wall."

They finally sit down after she has announced the contents and decor of the restaurant and the waiter, who has tensed as soon as he saw them come in the door, tries to take their order, but it all turns into a complicated rigmarole which Mif and I observe bemusedly. The waiter glances at us and rolls his eyes.

When the ordering is over we get into a conversation with her, or rather we listen as she tells us what Amarillo is like and what her children are like and what her husband does for a living. He, meanwhile, sits there pretending he doesn't know her and that it is just some weird twist of fate that finds him sitting at the same table. As she is talking, a brand-new magenta Coupe de Ville with a snow-white padded vinyl top and an opera window pulls up out front with Washington plates. Through the screen door comes a middle-aged man with gray coiffed hair wearing a tailored and sequined suit, see-through shirt open to his hairy chest, silver and jade bracelets on

JIM CHRISTY

his wrists; accompanied by two women in high heels and short shorts, one of them sporting an ankle bracelet and blond Afro wig, the other wearing a glitter halter top and reeking of Charlie.

The lady from Amarillo looks up and actually drops a syllable. "Well, ah dee-clayuh!"

Burwash Lodge, Mile 1103... We spend the first night out of Whitehorse at Mr. Allinger's lodge, a veritable cliché of a mountain hostelry set right on Kluane Lake and at night from your window you can hear the thupping of the water as it hits shore and washes the gravel with a shoosh like brushes on a cymbal. At dawn and dusk the mountains on the other side of the lake are black cut-out forms against the dark pink-tinged sky. The cool lake air carries a hint of early fall wood smoke.

Before turning in we have a few drinks in the lodge's linoleum-floored bar where two helicopter pilots are getting too drunk to fly and one kid from Newfoundland keeps interrupting them to brag of his many fistic exploits, how he kicked this one and that one insensible. An old Indian man sits quietly sipping his beer and watching Mif and me.

After a while he smiles and nods his head at us, invites us to join him. When we are seated he remains absolutely still and silent for a couple of minutes and then he says, "I want to tell you a story about something that happened years back to my cousin. This cousin, he owed lots of money to the trading post here at this place here, called Burwash. He was an honest man my cousin, just like me and hard-working too. Not very much like me. The trader, he knew my cousin was honest and so he give him more credit. But my cousin he could not make any money no matter what he done and to make it worse his old wife dies in the middle of the winter. He was very sad but because it is winter he could not dig a hole to bury her. So he hauled her body up into a tree. When he did this it made all the animals come around. All the animals in the forest come to the tree to prowl there in the nighttime and sniff at the body. So my cousin he set his traps there by the tree and he had his best season ever. He made enough money to pay the trapper and he had plenty left over. And that's what happened to my cousin."

America!

Alaska!

Where the future is.

No sooner do they finish building one pipeline than they start on another one. Land of the six-thousand-dollar-a-month welding job. Waitresses who dabble in real estate. Gold nugget watches on the arms of boys a year off the farm. Fairbanks! One of the few places on God's earth where you will find Eskimo men wearing mascara. Money, oil, gas, snow, whores, and Teamsters.

And to think that the American Secretary of State got Alaska from Russia for $7,200,000 and they laughed at him. Called it Seward's Folly. It was pigeonholed as Indian territory and promptly forgotten about until the Gold Rush. Why, in 1868 the people of Sitka, fearing a native uprising, had to call on the Canadian Government for help.

What a wonderful, heartrending feeling it must be to stand just over the border and look off across the broad plateau into the horizon with Fairbanks just beyond and to know you've driven that nine-year-old Fury all the way from Alabam where things had ceased to look so grand in Birmingham; you, the missus, the three kids, the furniture in a U-Haul and roped to the roof. The springs of the Fury groan under the weight of human hopeful flesh and the impedimenta of living.

I have, no lie, seen men drive through customs, stop by the side of the road and kiss the Alaskan asphalt.

They are thinking, We made it, sweet goddamn. Maybe this time we'll find it. If it's anywhere it has got to be here. The missus is thinking the same thing despite her previous doubts through the rough unpaved Canadian passage. The words of a song keep echoing in her head, the ones about following him to Utah and Nebraska and it never working out, and finally reaching Alaska where there was sure to be a gold mine.

It is just like the Okie migrations to California in the thirties. Old cars with southern plates loaded down with hope. Tired of being busted down and busted out, working in the sawmill, working in the fields, working on the line. Fresh out of the Army, fresh out of jail. Looking for a new start. During the main rush to Alaska, at the height of the North Slope Pipeline project, grown men were getting paid $2.50 an hour in the southern states and in California too, where the minimum wage had not increased in over ten years. In 1979 it is $2.65.

You see the old jalopies wedged in between tourist Winnebagos in the summertime. Whole families asleep in blankets or patched canvas tents far enough off the road to avoid the dust. Families with serious purpose. Young kids off on a lark, out for big bucks and a good time, and waiting down on Second Avenue are hookers who take charge cards.

The road for the rest of the journey cuts through the broad plateau between the Wrangell, Nutsotin, and Alaska mountains with the Brooks Range far to the north. The mountains seem to lurk on all sides, often just faintly visible on the horizon but always felt, always there in the distant haze, as if to not let you forget your own humble human insignificance, tiny specks inching across the vast floor of the Tanana River Valley. The many creeks form crevices in the bottom of the valley bowl and it is here in the fissures that the alder and the cottonwood, the willow and the aspen, proliferate. Stream margins with water hemlock and purple violets. Between the creeks and rivers buck brush dominates and the sunlit meadows are brilliant with yellow milk vetch and blue gentian. Even the old Alcan drainage ditches seem to be on fire with thousands of tall yellow duster flowers.

Tetlin Junction, Mile 1311, the cutoff for the Top of the World Highway to Eagle, Alaska, and Dawson City, Yukon. There is a lodge and truck stop here and four log cabins with wood-burning stoves. The truck stop features the world's coolest gas station attendant. A thin, curious Inuit hipster with a pencil-thin mustache and a low, wise voice. "Wow. Say, man, where you headed?... Fairbanks, hmmmm... well, groovy."

He glides around the gas pumps, head bowed, humming to himself. He fills the tank and snaps his fingers. I go around to watch him. He is—I don't believe it, so I lean close—he is scat singing. "Shoobee, dewop, skiddy op, shoo bop."

What is *he* doing here? Or rather, what is he *doing* here? What's his story? I wish I had the month to stick around and find out. I try to engage him in conversation. "I'm hip. I'm hip," he assures me.

He is well into his forties, looks like a gaunt old-fashioned junkie. I can just picture it: as a kid he probably attended a Catholic mission school in some place like Barrow and his life was changed irrevocably when one night creeping around the rectory log cabin he overheard one of the good father's bop records on the wind-up Victrola. He recognized immediately the similarity with old Eskimo songs, same atonal polyrhythmic sound. He started singing to himself improvisations of the old songs, like Lester Young turned loose on seal-hunting chants. He asked questions and the father told him stories. "Right this very moment somewhere far away in the mainland a cat with a tenor is standing on a stage and everybody is going wild listening to him make this music, same as you're listening to now."

He decided right then to head out for L.A. to see palm trees and hear Wardell Grey. Maybe he made it and bought a zoot suit and fell by clubs on Central Avenue posing as mulatto. Listened to cool jazz, bought a tenor with sticky valves and smudged adhesive tape over the cracks, practiced in his hotel room, and when he was good enough decided to go back to the Arctic barrens and start a weird bop Eskimo band.

But for some reason he never made it past Tetlin Junction. He lives in one of the log cabins back of the restaurant, moth-eaten zoot suit packed away in a duffel bag stored under the bed, and blows his tenor late at night when he is all alone out by the gas pumps.

Crazy.

In the restaurant: big mugs of coffee, homemade cinnamon buns and apple pie, greasy large portions of food and a huge woman cook in filthy apron. The truck drivers keep segregated from the car drivers. They discuss their routes, their companies, that idiot in a Volkswagen camper that stopped in the middle of the highway down in Sedro Woolley, and the flash of beaver on the four-lane outside of Anchorage.

In the men's washroom, written on a wall:

God made that road out there to punish truckers

and

Driving for K&W is like friggin a hog
It ain't too bad but
You just don't like to talk about it.

On the other side of the café at a table are an elderly gent and a young boy and it is plain to see that they are enjoying themselves immensely. Mif and I start talking to them. Granddad and a kid. They're coming from Indiana—what a trip—just the two of them in an eleven-year-old Falcon, trunk filled with fishing gear and camping equipment, glove compartment crammed with maps and marshmallows, dashboard cluttered with sunglasses, Life Savers, chocolate bars, and cookies. The old man laughs all the time and tells stories while the kid looks at him with the utmost admiration and flat-out adulation. "Took me three years to convince his Mom and Dad to let me take him along. Especially since my wife wanted no part of the trip."

No wife to keep the old man reined in. No parents to mete out discipline and worry about where to stop, and to divide the kid's attention. They are buddies and equals, the way fathers and sons can never be. The old man begins a story about a bear that hung around their cabin in British Columbia and it dovetails into a yarn about when he used to raise pigs back in Indiana, seventy miles from the Indianapolis Speedway. The kid interjects about the honest-to-God Mountie they saw back in the Yukon and the old man sputters, "Mountie, yep that's right. And the bear. Don't forget the bear. Big old bear he was too. Yes. Heh, heh. Want a milkshake? That's right!"

They stop jabbering long enough to pay the bill and the old man says good-bye and to the kid, "Let's go do some fishin'," and off they go, tumbling into the old car. Driving off, the old man talking himself blue in the face, sputtering chocolate chip cookie crumbs all over the dashboard. The kid proud as can be because the old man is the world's greatest fisherman and woodsman and buddy and absolutely the No. 1 Granddad.

Mile 1314 ... Tok, Alaska ... A roadhouse Saturday night. Rockabilly and raucous behavior going on in Young's Husky Lounge. The band is wailing, the dance floor is crowded, and they're wedged four deep at the bar, hands pass along money and beer in aluminum cans like at a ball game. The men are construction workers, oil men, dog mushers, and breeders. The women work in local lounges and restaurants or actually live here all year around and have regular homes and families. Tok is dog-raising country. People talk dogs or nostalgia. The action and conversation start the minute you walk in the door, and don't stop until you leave. A little bit of culture shock after a thousand miles of Canadian waterholes where unless people are totally drunk they tend to be reserved. This is the kind of place where someone is going to talk to you and for no reason other than a little companionship. The guy on the next stool is either going to turn out to be your best buddy or take a swing at you. Either way, you will know you're alive.

Mif has been asked to dance ten times before she can finish her first drink and I've already made a couple of great friends and taken down a few addresses. "You ever come through El Paso, you look me up, hear?"

The fellow on the stool in front of me, whom I can't help leaning against from time to time in the general jostle and activity, looks like Lloyd Bridges and tells me he's a construction foreman. Buys me a Schlitz and allows as how he's homesick for Michigan. Can't wait until January and shutdown time so he can get back home. "I got ten acres with the nicest little house on it and the best trout stream in the world running through the middle of the property. Boy, oh boy!"

Trout! Lord, man! This is the *land* of trout streams. But nostalgia is the best fishing hole of all. Nothing like a trout caught back home in the land of big two-hearted rivers. Hem fishing the dark pools in the early morning.

Our words on fishing back home start the big guy on the other side of me talking about his home, which is a farm in Iowa, and as a matter of fact he looks like Central Casting's Iowa farmboy. Looks like Randy Quaid, which is the same thing. Tall, husky, round-faced and jug-eared, an expression of simple concerns, wide-eyed, wearing a cap with a Purolator badge. He's a salesman of oil filters and travels all around Alaska. Used to be a tackle on the high school football team.

Someone comes over and insists on introducing me to his boss and his wife. A huge Indian drapes his arm over my shoulder and swears we worked together on a job somewhere and insists on buying me another Schlitz to remember the occasion.

The band keeps working. The beer keeps flowing. Backs are being slapped. It's a good-time scene save for one fellow brooding over by the doorway, a weight-lifter, obviously. Sleeves cut out of his tight sweater, he flexes his muscles and glares at any male who catches his eye. Everyone ignores him and he slinks off into the night.

Mif and I dance long into the early hours of the morning and leave at 3 A.M. and outside a man we never saw before says he hopes we had a good time.

The Sunday morning-after breakfast takes place at the little log cabin diner at the Glenn Highway Intersection. I recognize people from the bar. There is a serious nursing of hangovers going on at some tables: bowed heads, red eyes, trembling cups of coffee, hands fumbling in shirt pockets for cigarettes. Unmindful of this sober adult state of affairs, three teen-aged workers with Texas accents come in laughing and kidding each other about what they did the night before and all the time mock-groaning, "Man, I got me a bee-ug haid this mawnin'."

They order huge breakfasts of hotcakes, bacon, eggs and hash browns, and on top of the mound of food dump blobs of ketchup, causing grown men to look away.

"Hay-ul, I thought chew was gittin' sweet on at lil blonde last nide, Larry."

"Damn, Warren, he warn't neither. Din't you see him makin' up to that ole squaw?"

Outside, kids are lining up in the morning hitchhiking positions. At the junction is Dennie's Speed Kleen, a laundromat in the form of a monstrous, three-story-high washtub. The Texans finish breakfast and have to get to work. They are all overgrown and gawky and coordination hasn't caught up with them. They rush out bumping into tables and chairs like overeager puppies, climb into two low-slung Fords with glass pac mufflers and pull away, spraying gravel on Ma and Pa's camper.

Johnson River, Mile 1380…After driving the '67 Chevy three hundred miles over rocky rutted Canadian road, it decides it can't take the smooth asphalt of civilization (relative) and blows a tire. The jack is rusted and useless. We sit by the river and wait for someone to come along.

A vehicle appears after half an hour, a yellow Datsun pickup, and I wave it down. Two long-haired, bearded, back-to-earth types in their mid-thirties get out in overalls and rubber boots. I borrow their jack and set to work while Mif tries to engage them in some conversation. They are not unfriendly but as taciturn as a pair of elderly New England farm brothers.

One eventually breaks the string of "Yeps" and "Nopes" to allow as how the pipeline is ruining Alaska by bringing in too many people and if there is one thing he hates, it is too many people. When I'm finished I thank them and they nod and drive away ever so much like a cooled-out version of the Freak Brothers.

Twenty miles farther on, way back off the highway down a muddy lane, I spy a cluster of trailers and a barn-like garage surrounded by twenty or so junk cars. I turn down, half thinking I might get a tire off one of the wrecks and half out of curiosity. In front of the garage is a craggy-faced man in permanently begrimed coveralls trying to get a school bus started. He emerges from inside and plunges his hands into the innards of the bus motor. Blackened, swollen hands, grease that will never come out from the cracks in his fingers. He tells me he came to Alaska from the countryside near Covington, Kentucky, worked on the pipeline for a year, taking but a day or two off, and bought this place with his earnings. His two little boys hang around handing him tools and asking questions. A tall and jolly, florid-faced fat man comes over, nipping at a back-pocket pint of Bourbon and bends to study my Yukon license plate. "Lawd, lawd," he drawls, "a Canadian boy. You don't *look* Canadian."

He laughs and I wonder what the hell he means by that.

"What the hell you mean by that?" I ask.

He finds my question even funnier and says, "Just never you mind. Never you mind."

I take the proper size tire off a dead Fairlane and note that some of the junked cars are from Illinois and Georgia. They had penetrated far enough into the land of the future that when they expired their owners could not be too angry, just gave them a final push into the woods or else, broke, their drivers pulled in here and sold them for bus fare into Fairbanks. Where do they start their auto-biographies, these old wrecks all lachrymose in junkyards, once fine sedans, squatting ignominiously in the roadside weeds?

Delta Junction, a town that vigorously insists it, and not Fairbanks, 101 miles away, is the end of the Alaska Highway. It is here that the Alaska Highway joins the Richardson, Alaska's first highway, for the final leg into Fairbanks. The U.S. Army Corps of Engineers did not have to build past Delta Junction, therefore, claim the town fathers, we are obviously the end of the road. On the other hand, the Alcan wherever possible was built over previously existing trails and stretches of actual road. And furthermore the goal of the project was Fairbanks and the dramatic factor must prevail and declare for it and not Delta Junction.

The town, which stretches for miles along the highway, began in 1919 as a work camp for the Richardson, itself built over an old sixteen-foot-wide pack trail connecting Valdez on Prince William Sound with the gold fields at Eagle and Fairbanks. Bison from Montana were imported here in the twenties and the settlement was known until the building of the Alcan as Buffalo Center.

Rainier and Olympia beer signs are glowing in the window of the Club Evergreen hard by Mary's House of Beauty (*"Ladies Fresh Up! It's the End of the Alcan"*) and inviting us to enter.

Now what better way to meet the people and get the true feel of these little communities than by visiting the local watering holes, which are the social and business centers after all? Drinking is a big part of the life of the North, some would say the biggest part, and a teetotaler knows not the land of the midnight sun. Belly up to the bar if only for a coffee or a club soda. Had you not stopped, you would fail to be introduced to any of the gallimaufry of types known as Alaskans and proud of it.

Jeanie the bartender, for instance, of the push-'em-up bra, blond bouffant hair, and painted green eyelids.

"I'm from Arkansas, Little Rock, but I consider myself to be an Alaskan now. I spend my winters here."

She rode the bus North but ran out of money when she got to Calgary, where she had to "Um, work for a while." When she had enough together she bought another bus ticket, this one to Fairbanks.

"The bus stopped for half an hour at a place called Pink Mountain in British Columbia. The lady there waiting on tables was pregnant and I could see right away that she was feeling sick. She fainted right in the middle of serving a whole busload of passengers. Her husband was taking care of her and just got up, found an apron, and went to work. Stayed four months."

When she got to Delta Junction she fell in love with it and decided she was going no farther. "I wouldn't go back to the States for anything." She is a splendid bartender and can earn a lot of money. "Besides, it's so much fun dancing at all the lodges hidden away in the woods on the lakes. Tourists don't know about them. In the winter we all get plastered and play snowshoe baseball. You ain't an Alaskan unless you've played snowshoe baseball."

I order another Wild Turkey. Soldiers from Fort Greeley are shooting pool. A young girl comes in assisting her father, a man in his sixties crippled by arthritis. She helps him onto a bar stool, kisses him on the cheek, and leaves him there. It is obviously a daily ritual. "The usual, Jeanie."

She brings him a Southern Comfort. We get to talking and he tells us that he arrived a year ago from Vincennes, Indiana, to be near his two sons, one a minister in Fairbanks, the other a pipeline worker. The skin on his hands is drawn tightly over the misshapen knuckles, the veins stand out vulnerable and blue. He cradles the glass in a clawlike grip. He begins to talk about music and as it turns out he used to be a bass player in Les Brown's Band of Renown. "I wanted to make music my life but ..." he sighs, looks at his hands and leaves the sentence unfinished.

Tanana River... an Alyeska Pipeline camp. The welders are up on high scaffolding fitting a giant elbow pipe into place. Little kids watch them from behind the chain-link barbed-wire-topped fence. On the shore people are beaching their Alaska river boats—thirty-foot-long freighter canoes with huge twin Mercury outboard engines. An American Colette, a lady with pancake makeup, rouged cheeks, garish kohl eyes, and henna hair, sits in the passenger seat of a camper stroking a Siamese cat with robin's-egg-blue eyes.

The Tanana River is the inspiration for the great Alaskan annual betting classic with one hundred thousand dollars in prizes for those who guess the day, hour, and minute that the river ice will break up and start to move downstream.

Twenty miles along the road is the Richardson Roadhouse, which advertises it has "sassy help." It is one of the original log cabin inns that were built every twenty miles along the old trail. The prospectors and trappers would stop here, traveling by horse, foot, bicycle, dog team, or in old Studebaker sleighs with carbon heaters at the foot.

Twenty miles from Harding Lake and just past the Boondox Bar there is a curious two-story building whose walls bear a forest mural with bear cubs shimmying up a tree and fish jumping in the streams. The shades are drawn over the windows. What could it be? We stop to explore.

A strange lady appears and invites us in for coffee. She has a severely lined face, eyelids like walnuts, and her iron-gray hair is arranged in a disconcerting Veronica Lake peek-a-boo style. She is in her middle fifties, diminutive, active, speaks out of the corner of her mouth. She says the place is for the elderly.

"Where are they?"

"That's the problem, sweetie. I run it for the old people but the city has stuck it way out here twenty-five miles from town where the rent is cheaper but where the old people can't get to it. They don't give me any money for upkeep. I haven't gotten paid for two months. But if I don't do it, who the hell will? Personally, I make out. I got a place down the road. I raise dogs."

She chain-smokes Camels, slits her eyes to exhale smoke through her nostrils. She tells us she came from St. Louis in the early forties with her new husband who was a Navy pilot. "He had the choice of here or Hawaii. I wanted him to take Hawaii. But, no, he was fascinated by the Jack London bit. We were here three months and he died in a crash over the Aleutians. The poor bastard. I just stayed on."

We talked and drank coffee with her for another hour and left her there sitting alone in the darkened old folks' social center on the other side of the forest walls.

North Pole ... the last community before Fairbanks. Originally a homestead site, it was bought out by a development company that named it in the hope of coaxing a toy manufacturer to relocate because of the advantage of a North Pole address. The ploy worked. A man named Con Miller runs Santa Claus House and is widely known and well loved because he not only sends Christmas gifts to poor children in remote Alaskan settlements but also answers all those letters kids from around the world write to "Santa Claus, North Pole."

Nevertheless, the little community seems dedicated to the motto: When you've got a good theme, flog it. Homes and businesses are decorated for Christmas twelve months of the year. There is the Snowflake Laundry, North Pole Trading Post ("*Santa's Christmas Home*"), Arctic Acres subdivision, KJNP Radio ("*The Gospel Station at the Top of the Nation*") whose staff live free in log cabins in "Jesus Town." And on the local pop station Roy Helms' "Jingle Bell Rock" is in the top forty all year round.

Four miles from Fairbanks a line of gray fighter planes stand poised and ready before their hangars at Fort Wainwright.

Then the outskirts of town, a cluttered jumble of pre-fab and franchise, a miasma of drive-ins, shopping centers, warehouses, motels, and vacant lots—once parcels of the Tanana Valley wilderness, now civilized with oil cans, tin cans, McDonald's wrappers, old tires, last month's centerfold, and the remains of a microbus from Mississippi—all making the city limits vaguely reminiscent of the back of an old radio.

THE ALASKA HIGHWAY runs into Cushman Street and on into town. On Second Avenue black hookers in blond Afro wigs parade, shaking the shakable, showing the stuff, licking frosted lips with pink tongues, and offering fake lascivious leers to short-haired, fresh-faced soldier boys. The pimps are draped over the bar in places like The Mecca and The Golden Nugget. The big parking lot is filled with dented Jeeps, mud-splattered campers, hillbilly Fords, old Volvos owned by geologists, and long cream-colored Coupe de Villes. Kids lie around in sleeping bags, their heads propped against tires. Over in a corner of the lot behind a van a couple of people are completing a deal of some kind while Eskimos pass around a bottle of California port a few feet away. Three pipeliners with beards and long hair and ample bellies commandeer the middle of the sidewalk, drinking beer and smoking cigarettes, tossing each dead Oly can into the street, vying with one another in exclaiming what they'd like to do to their section foreman. Down the street, tourists take photos of gold nugget watches in a jewelry store window and Indians in tattered clothes sprawl on the curb in front of them.

Several years ago, pre-pipeline, Fairbanks was acclaimed as an All-American city. Farther back, a hundred years pre-pipeline, the land on which it sits, the land that it litters, had never even been viewed by the white man's eyes.

Arthur Harper, a prospector, was the first white man down the Chena River, arriving in 1873. He found evidence of gold but he neither stuck around nor returned to the country because the gold would have been too expensive to bring out. Fifteen years later Lieutenant H.T. Allen went up the Copper River to explore the area for the United States Government and in 1898 Lieutenant Caster arrived at the mouth of the Volmar River and after four days into the country, determined that perhaps as many as ten men lived in the entire Chena Slough.

In 1901 Ebenezer T. Barnette of St. Michael traveled up the Chena in a little steamer, the *Lavelle Young*, with the intention of trading with the Indians. Five miles from the river's junction with the Tanana, Barnette put to shore to cut wood for the stoves. It just so happened that an immigrant Italian prospector named Felix Pedro was in the hills above and saw the smoke rising from the river. Pedro hiked down and made the acquaintance of Barnette. They were an unlikely pair. Barnette was a crook, an embezzler, a man whose name would become synonymous in Alaska with the more sneaky of swindles. Pedro had been put to work in the coal mines of his native Bologna when he was seven years old. The mines were all he knew—those in France and southern Illinois—until he reached the Cariboo gold fields in the 1890s. From there he drifted to Dawson and got out when it became too crowded.

Pedro told Barnette he felt in his bones that there was gold in the immediate vicinity of where they stood talking. Barnette had intended to establish his trading post at Tanana Crossing but he allowed Pedro to change his mind. For those who are familiar with Barnette's future and his past, it might seem out of character for him to trust in another man. Not so. If there was gold, there would be men to find it and, thus, men to steal it from.

It is Felix Pedro who is considered the founder of Fairbanks although its first name was Barnette's Cache. Pedro indeed found his gold the next year on a creek that feeds the Chena.

The area fell under the jurisdiction of Judge James J. Wickersham of St. Michael who named the town, which he had never seen, after his good buddy back home in Indiana, a senator and future Vice President of the United States, Charles Warren Fairbanks. In the spring of 1903 Wickersham felt it incumbent on him to take a look at the little settlement that was beginning to draw the gold-hungry from Outside. He journeyed by dogsled from St. Michael and found "sourdoughs and cheechakos, miners, gamblers, Indians, Negroes, Japanese, digs, prostitutes, music, drinking! It's rough but healthy—the beginning—I *hope* of an American Dawson."

In 1903, forty thousand dollars in gold was taken out and the Rush began. Dawson and Nome were drained. The real death knell for Dawson as a gold town was sounded when Cheechako Lil saw the writing on the wall and deserted for Fairbanks, where she set up shop on Second Avenue, thus beginning the city's proud tradition of prostitution.

Further strikes were made on Fairbanks Creek and Fox Gulch, at Chatman and Cleary, where a fair-sized town grew up. This was the first modern boom. Roads were built to the creeks and a telephone system installed. Towns arose at Dome and Ester. The Tanana River Railroad built track to Ester Junction and down to Fairbanks in 1905. A telegraph line connected Fairbanks and Valdez and a trail was built over the Thompson Pass through the Copper River Valley, a trail that eventually became the Richardson Highway and a hundred miles of the Alcan.

The next year, on May 22, 1906, most of the little city, the "largest log town in the world," went up in flames. But so great was civic pride that the rebuilding had begun before the last ember died. The day after the fire, surviving businesses advertised *"Genuine Fire Sale."* The town was rebuilt in a month!

There was a spirit of friendliness uniting the people that helped such hardships to be endured. Although, as Wickersham noted, the people came from everywhere, no one cared about whatever deeds lurked in their neighbor's past. As Rex Beach wrote in *The Spoilers*: "You was in trouble—that's unfortunate; we help you—that's natural; no questions asked—that's Alaska."

Now the descendants of these Tanana Valley pioneers can only sit and shrug and sigh at the antics of the new breed. Long-haired rednecks from Texas who put their pointy-toed boots to the hirsute heads of other rednecks just because they happen to hail from Oklahoma. Why, this fellow in the short-sleeve nylon shirt with the wrinkled face of an old Alaska hand got his gold nugget watchband in '47 before some of these new people were born. "They come up from the lower forty-eight and leave their broken-down cars on my lawn. They cry and complain and vow to kick ass because their union-ordained coffee break was cut short twenty-three seconds. I nursed my pick-up, ancient when I got it, for fifteen years and these characters tear the gears out of sixty-thousand-dollar Cats and walk away laughing. They don't give a good goddamn because they're working a cost-plus project. And all the parasites that are living off this money they make! The whores. Nothing I got against whores. Far from it. Whoring has always been a way of life in Fairbanks. But it's a different class of hooker up here. Like this summer you've probably seen that Winnebago with the Florida plates? Well, it's making the rounds of the camps along the Richardson from Valdez to here. Driven by two wops with shades from Miami and in the back they got four women, blond, brunette, redhead, black hair. All they want is your money and get out. Used to be an Alaska whore had a heart of gold. I remember the poem my daddy used to recite when he'd had a few; about a whore, it was.

> "Lottie went to the diggings;
> With Lottie we must be just:
> If she didn't shovel tailings—
> Where did Lottie get her dust?

"See it was all good-natured back in the old days, which aren't so long gone actually. It was prostitution and some might call it sinful but it was *personal*. Now it is in there and out, not a second to spare, *impersonal* like everything else. But they do take your *personal* check or your American Express card.

"Ah, these people, what do they care for this country? They'll make their twenty-four dollars an hour for as long as they can take it, and get out. Good riddance, but they leave mementos of their presence all about; each one of them has destroyed a little of Alaska before they leave. And what they done to the Indians. I used to go out on the trapline and work with them people. My life depended on them and theirs on me. We got along fine. They lived and made do beautifully out there in the back country. Now they lie on the floor in the washrooms of the white man's bars. Try and find one that could live out in the forests. Talk about whores, the white man turned the Indian woman into a whore and then they couldn't even earn money that way because the black women came up from Detroit and Seattle and drove the Indian woman off the street. Like that song by Jerry Mac and Mike Dunham says—'Alaska Soul,' it's called:

> "I see the drunken Native now and know why
> he thinks drinking's fun
> 'Cause booze sure helps to blind your eyes
> to what the white man's done.
> I'm going to Second Avenue, get drunk,
> forget the pain.
> Alaska! Alaska! Oh why'd they make you change?
>
> "Lord, lord, ain't it the truth."
> Are you listening, Yukon?

Mif and I were sitting in Herb's Bar while a fat fellow in his early thirties bragged to us about his numerous adventures and incredible exploits. He had served two rounds of duty in Vietnam and killed "about a thousand gooks" and fought as a mercenary in Africa, assisting "'bout the same number of niggers" out of this world. Then he had run his own charter-boat enterprise in Newport News, Virginia, after which he made a million dollars in real estate. Which all made it curious, to my mind, what he was doing working as a mere cook, even though his employer was "Alaska's best restaurant."

"It's the greatest and the best but nobody much knows about it 'cause we keep it a secret. Don't want the pimps and the pipeliners to find out about it. It's in a castle back in the woods and you got to fly in there by helicopter, dig it?"

"Uh huh."

"Lots of famous people come in there. Last month the Fonz, you know, Henry Winkler, was in there. He was up to do some big-game hunting. I took him out hunting with me 'cause I told him the local hunters and guides weren't worth shit. I took him out, made a man out of him. Showed him how to shoot a .303. Then I brought him into town and got him some dark meat."

"Uh huh."

He continued in this vein for another few minutes and then, unfortunately, he had to go off somewhere to "see someone about a big deal I'm putting over." A round of drinks appeared and I asked the bartender, the Vietnamese war bride of a Green Beret, who had sent them over.

"Why, Bennie did," she said in a tone that implied I was dumb for having to ask.

"Who's he?" I asked, looking around the bar.

"Oh, he juss leff. He say give you anything you want long as you here."

I inquired of the fellow next to me who this Bennie was. "Why, he's one stone-crazy dude from down around Paraguay way. Has so much money he don't know what to do with it. Makes ten thousand dollars a month on the pipe and may the Lord strike me dead right now if I'm not telling you the truth. Just the other evening fellow in here said a few words to him in Spanish. Bennie, he was so glad to hear his own language, he stuffed a handful of tens and twenties into that fellow's pocket."

Now I had the idea I might stay in Herb's as long as it took for Bennie to return. After all, the funds were running low, that old Chevy had gone through two tires and numerous quarts of oil getting here from Whitehorse, and I *can* speak a bit of his language and he *is* buying. Lo and behold, he did arrive an hour later but, alas, he was falling-down drunk. I threw some South American slang at him, he giggled, seemed to reach for his pocket, and passed out, crumbling to the floor.

Ah well. I went into the washroom and on the wall read this sentiment:

> Texans aren't all bad
> I met one last year
> that wasn't a faggot

From my pocket I took my magic marker and underneath these words scrawled:

> . . . Rex Beach.

Motel on Lacey Street . . . lobby filled with soldiers and oil men; women of shady repute hang around outside the doors. As we walked to our room we heard a radio playing country songs, the door was open and a man was sitting on the edge of the bed with his elbows on his knees and he was staring at a spot on the rug between his feet. Beside him the desk with the peeling veneer top; in front of the mirror were gilt-framed photos of a woman and some children. I thought of the poem by Kenneth Rexroth, "Blue Sunday":

The radio is breaking
Somebody's heart somewhere
In a dirty bedroom.

Around four in the morning I was awakened by a female voice screaming in the night. I got up and looked out the window. There was the sound of a truck door slamming and heels clacking. The voice cried out, "If you think I'm going to give you a blowjob you're crazy!"

Fairbanks!

More pollution than Los Angeles!

Home of the world's busiest McDonald's!

Modem shopping malls and housing projects alongside wooden false-front buildings and turn-of-the-century log cabins. Five highways besides the Alcan end here, as well as the Alaska Railroad. There is a flight a day from New York. A flight a day from Tokyo.

We drifted through hotel lobbies, sat in bars and cafés, drove down little back streets, and peeked around corners and wherever we went we encountered displaced persons after the big buck.

A young Eskimo boy with teased hair and painted eyes swishing down the midnight avenue. The North Carolina couple picking each other apart in the fantastic Mexican restaurant. The hordes of dirty-clothes working men. Oldtimers bemoaning passing time, remembering a long-dead Alaska. Okies pumping gas. The Jewish man running the Vienna Delicatessen with Aleut waiters. A crowd of Eskimos gesticulating under a street lamp outside a Bingo parlor. Men in Fairbanks formal attire—leisure suits—plotting big deals with Arabs and Japanese in the basement restaurant of the Chena View Hotel. Cottages with three-foot-high cabbages in the garden. Sad parking lots. And always the whores: young ones working the streets and lobbies; old ones turned to waitressing in greasy luncheonettes.

There it is at the foot of Cushman across the street from the Arctic Café on the banks of the Chena River: the final Alaska Highway marker. Before it are the same tourists you probably saw in Dawson Creek. Fairbanks, the terminus to the Alcan. The All-American town smack dab in the middle of the tawdry future.

The beginning of the Dream and the end of the Road.

This is the law of the Yukon and ever she makes it plain:
Send me not your foolish and feeble; send me your strong
    and your sane—
Strong for the red rage of battle; sane, for I harry them sure;
Send me men fit for the combat; men who are grit to the core;
Swift as the panther in triumph, fierce as the bear in defeat,
Sired of a bulldog parent, steeled in the furnace heat.

ROBERT SERVICE, *The Law of the Yukon*

Dawson City was full of ribbon clerks.

WILSON MIZENER

8

WHEN WE GOT to Tetlin Junction on the return trip we turned off the Alcan and onto the Top of the World Highway for the drive to Dawson City. It had just begun to rain and already the road had turned to mud. The rain water had collected in the ruts and potholes and spilled across the ungraded surfaces. Thirty miles along we saw parts of the old pack horse trail to the Wade Creek gold mines and soon the road began climbing up Fairplay Mountain. At the top you're at 5,700 feet and looking straight down. The water seemed to be rolling downhill faster than we were climbing. No guard rails, unbanked curves, we drove with our hearts near our throats as the Chevy twisted and skidded, creeping dangerously close to the edges as we went around many curves sideways.

At Action Jackson's lodge at the border we picked up a guy on his way back from the Alaska Panhandle where he had been working on the fishing boats. He was headed home to Oregon, where he did much the same thing. It took nearly 7½ hours to make the 150 miles and for the last half of it the guy sat in the back seat in a semi-lotus position calmly meditating, oblivious to the eternities of wilderness waiting thousands of feet over the side of the road inches from his window.

Finally at Policeman's Point we started the descent to the river and the ferry. Dawson City appeared as we crept down out of the clouds. A cluster of wooden buildings nestled between the river and the mountains, with Moosehide Hill standing guard at the far end of town.

The streets were deserted in the rain. We drove along Front Street past the Bank of Commerce where a young former drifter called Robert Service used to stand behind a teller's cage. Down the street a wet dog took shelter under the overhanging roof of the Downtown Saloon whose lights shone through the swinging door. There was a lull before the activities of Discovery Days when Dawson celebrates its gaudy past, about the gaudiest past any town anywhere can claim.

The town bursts into life on August 17 every year. The streets are jammed with tourist campers and every pick-up truck from five hundred miles around. Indians, miners, families from Colorado as well as the entire city of Whitehorse throng the dirt streets and elbow their way through Diamond Hall Gertie's, home of the only legalized gambling in Canada. I recognize old friends like Joe Nickel, former magician and private detective, manning the Crown and Anchor wheel. Bob Cusick, the Cat driver, in the middle of a 48-hour poker game. My old buddy Erling working as a doorman. The oldtimers are dressed in their best sourdough garb. Insurance salesmen from Hartford, Connecticut, snap their pictures. The girls are kicking their legs onstage, a lady in black fishnet stockings is tickling the ivories for a Gay

Nineties tune.

The Gaslight Follies are playing at the Palace Grand, which was built by Arizona Charlie Meadows in 1899 with the lumber from two sternwheel steamers. The bars are jam-packed with drinkers. All the Indians are in from the bush. A team of *National Geographic* writers and photographers mill about taking notes and pictures. A thin, quiet cowboy called Lee from Hinton, Alberta, feeds his quarters into the jukebox. The action goes nonstop for three days.

And then early in the morning on the fourth day motel bills are paid, tents are taken down, camps are broken, and the line of cars and trailers begins making its way out of town. All day the caravan lasts and on the fifth day Dawson City has reverted back to normal.

The first cold spell comes in the early days of September and Gertie's closes down, sending the dance-hall girls home to Vancouver, and the Gold City begins to turn its collar up and hunch its shoulders for the long winter.

MIF LEFT ON A PLANE and I stayed on in Dawson for two months unloading the supply truck that came up twice a week from Whitehorse and then delivering its sacks of mail and the supplies for the stores. The days grew short and cold and the first ice began to appear at the edges of the Yukon and the Klondike rivers.

In the evening I would walk the streets deserted now save for the men walking from their pick-up trucks to the bars. Three hundred people live there in the winter, the same number as in 1896 before the Rush began and Dawson was a tent city for the few recalcitrant gold-seekers and Indians. Yet there are all these houses, enough for thousands of people, and they all stand empty, collapsing, buckling on their foundations of permafrost. They are being reclaimed by the bush. There is an eerie sense of time to Dawson in the fall and winter as you look up a street at the decrepit buildings, the boarded-up Occidental Hotel, and the listing Red Feather Saloon and always Moosehide in the background, gouged out by mining operations and famous from photographs, and you realize that Dawson looks exactly the same as it did in '98, only the people are gone. Thirty thousand men and women once filled Dawson City, making it the biggest town west of Chicago, and it is as if they all went away in the night leaving only the buildings.

Your footsteps really do echo on the board sidewalks in the night. Ghosts lurk in the abandoned buildings.

On these streets mingled the most motley crew of characters ever to appear at one time on the same stage in history. Players in the last great gaudy Gold Rush. Canada's one flamboyant hour of strutting. How could one have been young in '98 and not made the trek to Dawson City?

Bob Henderson was a prospector with a big heart—a heart of gold, precisely—even if precious little of the metal turned up at the bottom of his pan. But he did all right. He was working a claim on Humber Creek and having a bit of luck. He had a buddy though named George Carmack who was well known for never having much luck at all. Henderson thought he might do Carmack a favor, so he sent word for him to come out to Humber and stake a claim. Carmack arrived with two Indians named Tagish Charlie and Skookum Jim. Carmack staked and the three men started making their way back home. On the other side of the hill from Henderson the three men figured they might have a cup of tea before heading back to their settlement. Skookum Jim took the teapot down to the creek, Rabbit Creek, to fill. He stooped down by the water's edge at a spot where a reef crossed the creek and the bedrock was exposed. There, shining up at him from the water, was a gold nugget. He called Cannack and told him to bring the frying pan. Garmack scraped the contents of a rock crevice just above waterline and, when he had washed it, found three ounces of gold at the bottom of the pan. He repeated the procedure and yielded three more ounces. Without a word to Henderson the men staked and hiked out to 40 Mile to record their claims. There, at Willy McPhee's Saloon, George Carmack emptied his leather pouch of gold dust onto the counter and said, "Boys, the drinks are on me. I'm rich!"

The greatest Gold Rush of all time had just begun.

They came from New England mill towns and Carolina cotton fields; they came from other strikes and other misses; some from farms and some from slums; fresh out of the Army, just out of jail. A rush not unlike the present-day one for Alaska except that the dream was of fabulous wealth and untold riches, palaces of nuggets lay in store and not a job and two cars in the carport, a snowmobile, and a charter flight to Hawaii. It was the last gasp of oldtime romance and adventure. They were *all* there in Dawson in '98.

They came by river and they came over the passes. It was rough going and hundreds lost their lives, although, as with the construction of the Alaska Highway, men senselessly gave up their lives. One of the chroniclers of the time—a former cattle driver in the Southwest who would go on to trade in Mongolia, in Tibet, and in China where he rescued the boy Emperor and restored him to the Dragon Throne, an adventurer named Fred Meyer Schroeder—wrote about packing a ton of supplies over Chilkoot Pass, then sliding down to Lake Lindeman on sleds with his partner. "We were desert rats but the idea was the same—catch as catch can, make do, learn quick."

But many didn't learn quick. They were ill equipped physically or mentally for the climb over the pass and the boat trip to Dawson and they perished along the way. The thousands who made it found waiting in Dawson City the sharpies, the con men, the dance-hall girls, and the whores, not all with hearts of gold, who wished to take from them what they had brought over the passes and what they dreamed of bringing back.

Those who found gold banked it in Jack McQuesten's Alaska Commercial Store. McQuesten had been in the country since 1873 and his place stored the miners' gold in canvas sacks, each with the owner's name, stacked like cordwood against the back wall. The clerk would find your bag, measure you what you needed, and toss it back against the wall.

Schroeder bought a scow, hoisted it up on pilings, and converted it into a restaurant specializing in moose nose dinners at $4.50. He also brought in horses along Jack Dalton's Trail from Pyramid Harbor and rented them to prospectors. He made far more money from his restaurant and his horses than he did from ten years of working mining claims.

Wilson Mizener, who in the twentieth century was to manage the welterweight champion of the world, Stanley Ketchel, become Broadway's Shakespeare of the Underworld, be a star figure—albeit a tarnished one—of the Florida land boom during which he sold underwater lots, and a co-founder of the Brown Derby in Hollywood, ended the nineteenth century weighing gold and dealing faro in Dawson City saloons.

Mizener had been singing in a Barbary Coast saloon when he heard of the strike, but he had no idea of going North and soiling his hands. He brought with him, over the Chilkoot Pass, his girlfriend, a sloe-eyed chorus girl named Rena Faro. She earned their stake as they traveled the pass, selling her charms to hordes of womanless gold-seekers.

During their stopover in Skagway, Mizener had sat at the feet of Soapy Smith and gotten inspired; not that he was bereft of the con man's inclinations: It was more like learning from the master. Soapy had been kicked out of Denver where the rackets were controlled by the Blonger Brothers from Quebec. Soapy decided he would invade and conquer Mexico. He got kicked out of that country and found his true province in Skagway, where he bossed the town before his untimely demise. Mizener was later to enshrine Soapy in his pantheon of heroes alongside Jimmy Walker, Bat Masterson, Jack Johnson, and Ambrose Bierce.

Mizener got a job as a gold weigher at Swiftwater Bill Gate's Monte Carlo Saloon, where he presided behind massive brass scales converting dust into poker chips, whiskey, and tricks. He had tried the various ruses for attracting gold dust. He grew his fingernails long, used grease in his hair. Finally he devised a more profitable if short-lived method. He would place a square of carpet at his feet and, after a few days of use, burn it to extract the gold. His own smelter process. Mizener was finally fired when Swiftwater Bill, a famous philanderer and former dishwasher in a Circle City roadhouse, realized he was running out of carpet.

Later Mizener dealt faro, using Rena as a shill. Sid Grauman in his memoirs related how Mizener became enamored of a chubby chorus girl called Nellie the Pig and, to win her favor, he robbed the local candy store.

Mizener was no stranger to the Dawson City jail or other jails, but he finally left the Klondike when the Mounties instituted a policy whereby the inmates would spend the days of their incarceration chopping wood. Wilson had long ago vowed never to work.

He ended his days at Booth 50 in the Brown Derby from which he dispensed the dialogue for Hollywood gangster movies. It was said he was grateful when death overtook him for he felt the world was growing far too normal.

But things had been far from normal on the streets of Dawson. It was as if the Gold Rush were an initiation rite that, if survived, opened the toll gates of the road to success, although it was usually a back road through dubious terrain. The ranks of hustlers would be swelled immensely by Klondike veterans. Well-known carnival owners, race-track directors, prize-fight promoters, real-estate swindlers, and general all-around entrepreneurs were then nameless among the hordes. It was in Dawson City that Tex Rickard promoted his first fight and an unknown malcontent named Jack London missed it because he was too lazy to leave his wintery cabin.

Not only was Dawson a rite of passage; it also was, for many who had made their mark, a swan song. As the twentieth century neared, bringing with it, all too clearly, a new and different world; some, inextricably linked with that older age, journeyed to Dawson for the final hour of the wild and woolly frontier.

For the last time Bat Masterson strapped on his guns before going to New York to chronicle Broadway. Wyatt Earp dealt a few cards. The Montana Kid, last of the guns for hire, walked the streets, an old man. Down on Front Street Captain Jack Crawford ran a shooting gallery. Crawford had fought the Sioux Indians on the Great Plains and had ridden with Buffalo Bill. Arizona Charlie Meadows came to the gallery to perform. He was supposedly the best shot of his time and was said to be able to split a bullet on a knife blade at thirty feet or put a bullet through the throat of a bottle and break the bottom without touching the neck. Calamity Jane herself was in Dawson to challenge Arizona Charlie in monumental contests. Miners and drifters would gather around to watch history and legend shoot it out on Front Street. Some would live to the fifties and tell their grandchildren, "I saw Arizona Charlie Meadows outshoot the great Calamity Jane in Dawson City back in

'98." To which their grandchildren would reply, turning from the television, "Who?"

Rubbing elbows with the miners, the hustlers, and the whores were the writers and the writers-to-be who were to nail the legend of the Yukon forever to the page. There were London and Service. Hamlin Garland and Rex Beach and Joaquin Miller, poet of the High Sierras and well-known self-aggrandizer who filed his newspaper reports and entertained the sourdoughs with tall tales. Miller had been in on another rush, that of the 49ers, and assured anyone who would listen that the Klondike Stampeders were soft compared with those who had ravaged old Johann Auguste Suter's territory.

Rex Beach had been a law student at the University of Chicago, where he played on the football and water polo teams. When word of the discoveries at Bonanza reached Chicago he wasted no time in taking off. "I wasn't afraid of the hardships. Freezing was far more pleasant than drowning playing water polo."

He worked for two years in the Klondike, mining, logging, and doing odd jobs at Dawson and Ramparts, Alaska. Beach had been thinking of writing some stories about his experiences but a friend, one who had studied literature, told him, "There's no drama up here, no comedy, no warmth. Life is as pale and cold as the snow. There won't be Twains or Hartes as in California, won't be colorful stories from this drab and dreary country."

Beach was discouraged from writing. He left the North at the age of twenty-four to take a job back in Chicago as a salesman of building materials. One day a few years later he came across an old Alaska friend who had just earned ten dollars from the sale of an article on the Yukon. "Here was news more incredible than the Klondike discovery. Paydirt on Michigan Avenue running ten dollars to the pan."

He started writing that night and soon sold his first story to *McClure's Magazine* for fifty dollars.

He wrote on the weekends and continued at his salesman's job, even making vice president. Not until his writing income matched his salary did Beach give up the security of his job. He finished his first novel, *The Spoilers*, which was sold to the movies and remade three times. Beach, who was to produce more Alaska novels, was the first writer to popularize the Klondike and fix it in the public imagination.

The great Klondike adventures of Jack London have all been disproved by now. He drifted into the Yukon and drifted out again at the first opportunity, thus his experiences were no different from those of thousands of other transients. He didn't explore the territory for years, befriending all the Indians, miners, and mad trappers. He didn't make his stake taking other men's boats through the feared Whitehorse Rapids. It hardly matters. For the name London is synonymous with the Yukon. Everything he saw and everything he heard from the lips of others remained fixed in his memory to be transmuted by his imagination. "I never realized a cent from any properties I had an interest in up there," London was to write. "Still I have been managing to pan out a living ever since on the strength of the trip."

The Yukon was the mother lode he would return to even when the paydirt was exhausted. Whenever he was in debt he would ransack his imagination to come up with another northern story. In 1898 he had met a young adventurer named Marshall Bonds and had been impressed with the exploits of his part Scots shepherd, part St. Bernard dog. He turned these brief hours with this dog into the *Call of the Wild*. Years later at the wretched end of his career, London would twice resurrect Buck in two horrible, iron-pyrite novels set in Hawaii, *Jerry of the Islands* and *Michael, Son of Jerry*.

When Jack London returned to Oakland in August of 1898 he had to pawn the $4.50 worth of gold dust he had brought back from Dawson City. He was now as poor as ever, yet richer than he knew.

London's Yukon novels and stories, with the exception of *Call of the Wild* and *White Fang*, are the worst things he did in a prolific career. Wilson Mizener, who had been on the same scene, made fun of the London school of Klondike fiction with "its supermen and superdogs, its abysmal brutes and exquisite ingenues." Others complained that his craft consisted of turning men into brutes and brutes into men.

It is true that he used the Yukon and its people as setting and stock figures for his theories of social Darwinism, yet he, better than anyone else, captured the bitter, frozen land and the warmth of a fire, the wind howling outside the cabin door, the struggle for survival, and the struggle among men stripped of the protective clothing of civilization.

Yet London made little room in his stories for the color and the characters who were as much a part of the Yukon of '98 as were the brutish miners and the ferocious dogs. Ambrose Bierce had written, "Nothing will come of the Stampeder. He is a world in the wind, a brother to the fog. At the scene of his activity no memory of him will remain. The gravel that he thawed and sifted will freeze again. The snows will cover his trail and all will be as before."

But the cynic of San Francisco had not taken into account a Scottish immigrant, a drifter named Robert Service. Service is the true laureate of the Yukon, a revered figure down to today in modern pipeline disco Yukon. Why, men who restrict their reading to bills and beer labels, and would think lowly of any living man who versifies, can and may recite Service all night. Should your literary tastes require poetry more sophisticated than that of the Bard of the Yukon, you would be advised to keep it to yourself when in the saloons of Dawson and Whitehorse. And if you mention the name Robert Service in any of these watering holes, smile.

Service had quit his job with a bank in Scotland to come to North America. He hoboed across the United States to the West Coast, where he spent a year doing nothing but drifting up and down California living on oranges and mission handouts. He was content to pass the time playing his guitar and reading Jack London's recently published fiction about the Yukon. He made his way to Canada and secured a position with the Canadian Bank of Commerce, which sent him to Whitehorse.

He led a quiet life in Whitehorse, working long hours in the bank and avoiding the bars. His main social activity was reciting poems like "Casey at the Bat" during gatherings of the town's middle-class citizenry. The well-known Yukon journalist Stroller White encouraged Service to write a long poem for a church social. "There's a rich paystreak waiting for someone to work," he told Service. "Why don't you go on in and stake it?"

The next day after the bank was closed and all the other employees had gone home, Service sat at his desk staring at the blank sheets of paper waiting for inspiration. He heard sounds of merriment coming from a bar nearby and wrote, "A bunch of the boys were whooping it up in the Malamute Saloon..."

Service rose from his desk and began pacing, searching for a theme and his next line. Suddenly he heard the loud retort of a pistol and he ducked behind a desk. The night watchman had fired, thinking him a burglar. Service had his inspiration. There would be gunplay at the Malamute Saloon. By 5 A.M. he had written "The Shooting of Dan McGrew."

He recited his new poem at the church social and when he was done, inspiration appeared again, in the form of an aged miner who said, "Here's a story London never got..." and proceeded to tell him about a prospector who cremated his partner. Service spent the rest of that night walking around the streets of Whitehorse brooding on the miner's story and came up with the line, "There are strange things done in the land of the Midnight Sun."

Robert Service was never part of the actual Gold Rush—he came to the Yukon a few years too late for that—yet he is its most revered and truest chronicler. As he was to write in his memoirs, "While other men were seeking Eldorado, they were also making one for me."

I STAYED ON IN DAWSON CITY working except for a five-day trip up the Dempster Highway with Erling and Bob Cusick. The Dempster begins ten miles from town and is now built to Inuvik and the Beaufort Sea. When we made our trip a rough road had been cleared up to the Arctic Circle boundary at the Eagle River. Cusick was out to get his annual moose and Erling and I were content to shoot grouse for our supper and generally catch up on old times.

The Dempster is bound to play a significant role in making the Yukon a Canadian province. It connects the Beaufort Sea with the Alaska Highway and the rest of the continent, opening up some of the most beautiful scenery in the world. Conservationists claim it will be the bane of wildlife—the moose, sheep, and especially caribou that abound in the surrounding lands.

The road bisects the caribou migration route. When traffic begins in earnest—the oil trucks from the Sea and the tourist vehicles—the Dempster will become a major transportation corridor. The conservationists insisted that the herds would be decimated, but the government points to the fact that caribou have been crossing the road since construction was begun twenty years ago without any apparent adverse effect. Time, however, will inevitably reduce the herds, as was the case on the Steese and Denali highways in Alaska.

But it was just as inevitable that the road would go through. The effect on the environment was not as drastic as it could have been because the Dempster was not a rush project. By 1960 forty-five miles had been built along the North Klondike River, and only twenty more in the next two years before construction was halted until 1968. Because there weren't construction crews employed in different areas and working simultaneously, there was no need of access roads for supply purposes.

After the first miles of forest the road opened up plains that gradually rose to plateaus and mountains with their serried, looping ridges marking the horizon. The scenery changed drastically every so often and before one could get used to the particular environment. Forests to plains to rolling dun-colored hills. Then alpine forests, which gave way to the strangest Max Ernst landscapes: flat tableland with eerie mesas rising like mysterious growths bubbled up from underground cauldrons. There was a stretch of strange peaks, white sulphur cliffs, brilliant white and dark red hoodoos thrusting out of their granite ramparts, solitary gray chimney peaks like the towers of medieval cathedrals far off in the distance, and one night we camped in sleeping bags and I woke at dawn to see the tumble of peaks black and silhouetted in the dim light like piles of rubble and ragged pieces of wall left standing after a bombing raid on a German city.

I tended to the cooking chores, filling the coffee pot with cold Klondike River water, frying bacon and eggs, toasting thick slices of bread at the edge of the fire. We just drove leisurely and stopped and hiked through the woods where we could, but usually on either side of the road there was muskeg and along one stretch where it covered the hills, variegated little flowers bloomed and clung to the bog tops so that for mile after mile the hills were brilliant red and purple domes under a cloudless blue sky.

Around four in the afternoon when the sun was setting we would shoot our grouse for dinner and I cooked them in a way that would make Jesse Starnes proud. We camped one night along the Ogilvie River, hunched around the fire in the cold and sipped brandy, pretending we were outlaws on the run in 1880. The next day we went up to the Arctic Circle boundary and saw the Canadian Army tents whipped by cold winds; the last construction of the season was being completed on the other side of the river. I vowed someday to come back and drive to Inuvik and on the return to put a canoe in there at the Eagle and follow the river to the Porcupine and on to the last settlement in the Yukon, the Indian village of Old Crow.

On the last day Cusick disappeared into the woods and got his moose. We ate the heart around the afternoon campfire and headed back to Dawson as a light snow was falling.

I saved enough money to fix the Old Chevy, which had been severely battered by the rocks of the Alcan and the mud and strain of the Top of the World Highway, and when the snow began to fly, I packed my summer clothes into a duffel bag, said good-bye to my friends and headed south for Whitehorse.

I was alone on the road save for the occasional White Pass ore truck whose drivers would offer the Yukon salute, which is an arc of the hand and forearm across the full width of the windshield. There was no radio reception. It was quiet. The tires hummed on gravel. Snow clung lightly to the lip of the forest. I rolled down the window and listened to the Klondike River racing icy gray alongside the roadbed. The mountains stood dark and clear against the wan blue sky. I moved along past Bear Creek and the Dempster cutoff and stopped at a lone cabin with an old glass-bowl hand pump out front to get gas.

After another hour or so I was crossing McQuesten River and then Moose Creek. The road branches off to reach the mining towns of Elsa, Mayo, and Faro but I kept right, crossing the Stewart River. Many's the time I had knelt by the side of the road at that junction waiting for a ride. I used to rent a cabin along with my friends Erling and Patti at Fox Lake, two hundred miles to the south. Every once in a while it seemed important to leave them alone, so I would just walk up the trail from the lake to the road and stick my thumb out at whichever car came first, whether headed for Whitehorse fifty miles away or Dawson two hundred and fifty miles away. It usually took three rides to get to Dawson from the cabin. The first would inevitably be with a geologist or camp cook who had been into Whitehorse to get supplies. He would leave me at a place like the Minto airstrip and I would then hook a ride with a White Pass driver, having to duck whenever another company truck hove into view because of insurance regulations and company spies. The driver would let me off at Stewart because they were going to the mines. There I'd wait for a Dawson City traveler to pick me up. Once, on the first of such trips, I wrote in my notebook:

> On highway #3 just over Stewart River Bridge, thumbing to Dawson City. Kneeling in the gravel... On the other side of the road the river broad and placid. Mountains carpeted by unbroken evergreen forest ... Two young women in a camper with Michigan plates just passed, smiled but no ride... the river is lined by poplar and elm glittering in this rare burst of sunlight... gravel sandbars... fifty-foot sheer cliff face in back of me... what time is it? Who knows? Who cares?... just opened the last of the truck driver's beer on a rock, sip, and wave to an Indian family going the other way in a truck.

I passed the lodge at Stewart's Crossing wanting to make some time. I figured on not stopping until Midway Lodge seventy-five miles down the road. Three miles past the river I came upon a man hitchhiking the other way. I slowed past, wondering what his story could be. I could tell he wasn't a Yukoner. He was tall and lean and dressed in a denim jacket with the collar turned up, his hair greased back like a rockabilly singer, and he looked to be in his mid-forties. He couldn't be going to Dawson—there was no work there this time of the year and he certainly didn't look like a miner.

He waved as I came close. I spun the car around and stopped. "Where you going?"

"Alaska," he said in a southern accent.

"You're sure going the long way around."

"This is the Alcan, ain't it?"

"Hell no. Where you coming from?"

"Got a ride this morning from Whitehorse. Fellow left me off down the road a piece."

"Well, that fellow was playing a trick on you. You're headed for Dawson and when you get there, the road back to the Alcan is only going to be open a few more days."

"Damn," he muttered resignedly without a trace of bitterness.

"You look cold."

"I am cold."

"Get in. There's a lodge a couple miles back. Let's get us a coffee and get warm."

I was cold too, the heater wasn't working and I had opened the window to listen to the river.

Over coffee and apple pie he told me he was from Arkansas and how he did a fair bit of traveling. "They call me the Arkansas Traveler," he said.

"Naturally," I replied. "Why you going to Alaska?"

He told me about how the world was going crazy. So crazy, in fact, that people thought *he* was crazy for noticing it. And when things got to that point, he figured it was best to be moving on. "Why, I walk alongside the road and kids in cars throw stones at me or try to run me down. The po-lease run me in just to be ornery. I've spent my life drifting and it's getting harder to do. Man ain't free down South. You hardly meet anybody worth talking to. I'm just an old hobo."

He mentioned some places he had been and things he'd done. He had ridden the rails and shipped out all around the world. I knew he would recognize the name of an old road buddy of mine, and he did. Knew him personally, in fact. "Floyd Wallace and me was good friends and I am proud to have known him."

"Have known him? What's he dead now?"

"I don't know for sure but he kind of disappeared and don't nobody know what became of him. Nobody's seen him. He didn't show up for the annual do down in Britt, Iowa. He was last seen in California, near's I can figure. But, you see, he's just done a disappearing act like this whole way of life is doing. I'm hoping I'll find Alaska is a little bit different."

"I hope you do."

"Fellow named Frisco Jack told me I should come on up. And to meet him in Anchorage, which is what I plan on doing. You wouldn't happen to know Frisco Jack, would you?"

"Yeah, I know Frisco Jack."

"Well then, we got a few things in common. If I run into him I'll say hello for you and if by any chance Floyd's around I'll remember you to him too."

"Yeah, do that for me, please. And good luck to you in Alaska."

"Thanks, pardner, I'll see you down the road somewheres."

He took a position at the edge of the parking lot with the river bridge over his shoulder and I waved good-bye and drove on south. As I traveled I thought about him chasing that fading dream. As the forests and the mountains and the lakes whooshed by outside the windows of my snug car I dwelled on some of the memories he had uncovered, and I thought back on old Floyd. Hadn't Basho written about "all the ancients who died on the road"? The Arkansas traveler was right, of course. If that old-fashioned honky-tonk, freewheeling life existed anywhere, it was in Alaska. But I have a feeling it doesn't really exist there either and that is more than a little bit sad.

I drove through the little settlement of Carmacks and an hour later passed Fox Lake, which I knew so well. A short while later I could see Lake Laberge over to the left and in twenty more miles I was turning back onto the Alaska Highway for the ten-mile drive to Whitehorse.

I had been in Dawson so long that Whitehorse with its fourteen thousand people looked like the Metropolis. Its lights glowed in the basin down Two Mile Hill and seemed to welcome me. I had dreamed of Whitehorse and its urban pleasures. I remembered Service's lines of 1905:

> *This is my dream of Whitehorse when 50 years have sped,*
> *As after the Roger's banquet, I lay asleep on my bed.*
> *I tottered along the sidewalk, that was made of real cement;*
> *A skyscraper loomed above, where once I remembered a tent.*

There were still no skyscrapers, but it was all the Gotham I needed.

My dad and a partner started Whitehorse Flying Service. The partner and a passenger crashed and everyone searched for a week and then gave up. There was little hope for the men but my dad thought maybe the plane could be salvaged. A week later a surveyor was on a hill near Faro taking a leak when all of a sudden he saw an explosion. It took two weeks for the plane to go up in flames. That ended Whitehorse Flying Service and about sums up the early history of flying in the Yukon.

BOB CAMERON, bush pilot

9

BACK IN WHITEHORSE I was to look up a bush pilot named Mike Fritz, who was going to take me out for some winter flying. A couple of months earlier I had gone out with Trans-North Turbo Air's chief of pilot operations, Bob Cameron, and had developed a true admiration not only for the life these fliers lead but also for the important, even heroic, jobs they do. I thought particularly of Les Cook, whom the Army Engineers remembered fondly and who was awarded a Legion of Merit medallion for his heroic rescue of a soldier in 1942 but who crashed and died before he could be decorated.

I had met Cameron at the company's Schwatka Lake float-plane base east of Whitehorse to accompany him in the single-engine De Havilland to Keele Lake on the Northwest Territories border. I was hooked from the moment I stepped into the little yellow and red plane and it started to heave back and forth as Cameron built up enough revs to take off. Then we were scooting along the surface like a hydro plane and began to rise ever so slightly off the water. Soon I had the breathless sensation of hanging still in space like a cartoon character the moment he realized he has dashed off the edge of the cliff. But we didn't plummet and kept climbing higher, banking to the left and circling Long Lake, rising ever higher over nameless ponds and streams.

Cameron is a stocky man in his mid-thirties and that day he was dressed like your real Yukon bush pilot in old-fashioned black leather flier's jacket and chrome-edged sunglasses. We flew north between Mount Joe and Mount Byng, where in late August there was snow in the passes and on the high plateaus. We crossed the Teslin River toward the Sawtooth Range and the bigger Salmon Range of the Pelly Mountains. Cameron chewed his Dentyne and we shouted back and forth across the roar of the motor about the early days of Yukon flying, the roots of the tradition he loves and is very much a part of.

The tradition goes back as far as 1900 when John Leonard, "the Aeronaut," gave balloon-parachuting exhibits in the Yukon. Leonard's manager was none other than Captain Jack Crawford, who owned the shooting gallery in Dawson and had years earlier organized the first balloon spectacles in the United States. Leonard was wined and dined in Dawson and presented with a gold medal, token of the Klondike's esteem, by Frank Slavin, bouncer at The Monte Carlo and British Empire heavyweight boxing champion of the world.

But Leonard traveled in a balloon and not a plane and therefore Cameron, who is somewhat of a purist and who diligently researches the history of northern aviation, is not all that interested. He traces his own lineage to the likes of C.L. Prest, the first barnstormer to arrive in the Yukon. Prest was flying to Alaska in a ninety-horsepower biplane and landed at Whitehorse on July 8, 1922.

The first planes in the Yukon had arrived two years earlier. They were four open-cockpit De Havilland biplanes from the Black Wolf Squadron of the U.S. Army Air Service on a flight from Mineola, New York, to Nome, Alaska. A landing field had been hastily prepared above the town by a man named Mike Cyr who used an ax and crosscut saw to fell the trees, leaving the stumps flush with the ground. Thus the Whitehorse airport was born.

Prest was typical of the barnstormers, a daredevil ex-motorcycle racer, an Air Age swashbuckler. "Birdman Lands at City" headlined the Dawson *Daily News*. After being feted in Dawson, Prest was off to Fairbanks. He disappeared somewhere beyond Eagle, Alaska, and the papers gave their front pages over to the story. This Eagle-to-Fairbanks route was to come into prominence a few years later when it claimed the life of Will Rogers and Wiley Post. Prest had crashed but he survived to become a hero all over again.

The peaks of the Sawtooth Range lay ahead dark and gray and foreboding in the fog-bound distance. I couldn't help but think that although this wasn't exactly seat-of-the-pants flying it was still very much a gamble. There is no radio contact beyond a certain distance past Whitehorse. It is map-and-compass flying with small room for inaccuracy.

There is that particular excitement that comes with the intimation of danger and stimulates these pilots, and if they won't admit it for whatever personal reasons, they won't deny it either. I realized there was more than a little truth in the clichés about freedom of the skies and the abandon of the wild blue yonder.

"It gets in your blood and stays there," Cameron said, and as proof offered the example of Cedric Wah, a Chinese Canadian who began flying in World War II with Chennault's Flying Tigers. His job was to cart silver dollars over Communist lines to buy mainland allegiance. Wah was once forced, because of engine trouble, to dump forty million dollars in U.S. currency into the snows of the high Himalayas. Later, he worked as a bush pilot in the Yukon, saved his money, and invested it in Vancouver real estate. "Cedric became a millionaire a few times over," Cameron concluded, "but still returned to the Yukon every summer to fly for regular bush pilot pay."

On that first flight, Cameron and I were at 7,850 feet passing between granite-walled mountains topped by purple and green lichen. Jagged peaks appeared through the clouds below as if from out of a great smoking cauldron. Cameron talked of rescue missions. TransNorth evidently spends a fair amount of time going out and bringing back lost pilots, usually Americans.

"Americans fly by beams," he explained. "They can flick off frequencies just like that, but they come up here and there are no beams. They can't map-read so they try to follow the Alaska Highway and they get lost. Amazingly enough we only lose a few each year. We find most of them at Carmacks. They ask us"—and here Cameron assumed a southern accent—"'Where the hay-nil is Wide-Horse?'

"We passed Dragon Lake and a little farther, beyond the right wing, saw the few buildings and small airstrip that make up the desolate settlement of Twin Creek, infinitesimal in the vast mountainous world. The Macmillan River is surrounded by bald peaks, with mountain sheep clinging to the icy patches on top. We followed the jade-green Hess River and finally saw Keele Peak, the highest in the area at almost ten thousand feet.

We made a sweep before the mountain and threaded our way along a narrow twisting passage through the granite walls with literally only feet to spare on either side of the wings. The winds buffeted the little plane and Cameron guided us through the cavernous maze calmly chewing his Dentyne. Then suddenly we were behind the peak and there was Keele Lake in its awesome stillness.

We put down at the edge of the water before the outfitter's camp, which consisted of a log cabin surrounded by tents and a makeshift corral. The outfitter, Werner Koser, and his Indian wrangler were out with the ten hunters from the States who had paid generously for the privilege of hunting in territory that few other people had ever seen. We were greeted by Koser's wife, Elsa, and their daughter. A rack of caribou horns was mounted above the cabin door. We went in for a cup of coffee and to wait the arrival of the man we were bringing out. A couple of hound dogs slept in the dust in front of the door. Everything was perfectly quiet except for the rushing of a stream that emptied into the lake a hundred yards from the cabin.

After a few minutes the helicopter arrived and dropped off its passenger, a prospector and geologist named Al Higgins. He was on a reconnaissance mission for a Houston, Texas, mining company and had camped a few miles on the other side of Keele Peak.

We didn't have enough fuel to make it back to Whitehorse so we had to put down at a seaplane base near Ross River. After the Norman Wells pipeline and refinery closed down, Ross River was revived again as the site of the Anvil Mine, largest of Yukon mines. It was discovered by Al Kulan, who was one of the few white men in Ross River. After the strike Kulan bought a Rolls-Royce and he used it the same as he would a Jeep. You would see him driving around, the Rolls filled with picks and axes, grizzled miners and Indians. A couple of years ago he sold it for a normal vehicle. "Rollses," he said, "are overrated."

Rumor has it that Kulan was tipped on the Anvil site by an Indian named Joe Ladue. Kulan gave him a few shares as a reward but Ladue gave them away for booze. The bitter irony is that a couple of years later Ladue was killed in a head-on collision. The other vehicle was a truck from Anvil Mines.

The base was on a small lake surrounded by scrub bush and infested with mosquitoes. There were plenty of barrels of fuel around the dock but no filtering device. Water gets into the barrels and has to be filtered out. Without the filter it was necessary to pour small amounts of fuel into a bowl and filter it through a piece of chamois that Bob kept in the cockpit for such emergencies. It was a long tedious job of work and while doing it you had to keep stopping to swat mosquitoes and to curse. It was a makeshift operation worthy of the days when improvisation was a part of bush flying. To Cameron I said, "Gee, Bob, it's just like the good old days, huh?" He wasn't amused.

A DECADE AGO Yukon charter companies had to get their pilots wherever they could. Most were seasonal and many worked on a retainer. During the summers TransNorth used to employ several European veterans of the French Algerian War but these able pilots weren't interested in Yukon winters. There was a dearth of cold-weather pilots trained for the mountainous terrain of the North. Mike Fritz can fly anything anywhere.

We are on TransNorth's only scheduled run, a daily flight to the mining town of Faro. The plane is a Twin Otter capable of carrying eighteen people but there is a strike in Faro and our only passengers are two Vancouver television reporters on assignment to cover the negotiations. It is a relaxed trip and although it is gray and cold the weather is fine and there isn't much turbulence. So relaxed is it, in fact, that Mike lets me fly the plane while he talks about his work.

Fritz is thirty-two years old, an articulate man who loves to fly planes. He discusses the harmony of perfect stick and rudder use like an opera lover describing his big trip to Milan. He talks about line-of-sight flying and generally theorizes on force, thrust, and air currents. Then he moves on to avionics. It is a tribute to his powers of elucidation that if he does not exactly make it all seem simple to a novice, he succeeds in demystifying the dynamics of flight.

Mike is an example of the new breed of Yukon bush pilot, a resident Northerner, an exceedingly well-trained and full-time pilot. An Air Cadet flying scholarship enabled him to obtain his private license, and in 1965. he began flying commercially as a bush pilot in northern Ontario. He worked for three years taking fishermen, hunters, and tourists into the bush. In 1968 he moved to British Columbia to work for Northwest Air. He flew float planes and soon took over as manager of the company's Powell River base. He came to the Yukon to work for TransNorth in 1972.

The mountains seem made of the same substance as the clouds. It is a timeless snow-white netherworld existing outside all earthbound imaginings. The weather had suddenly turned bad near Faro and Mike had taken over the controls. We have had to come in high over the mountains and our descent is steep. It is like a rude return to the world after an exalted opium dream. There is the little town with its buildings dotting the gray-green, ice-clotted river. Tiny toy trucks inch along the neat dirt paths as if guided by the invisible hand of a child. We circle the mine on the hill above the town and come down on the gravel strip, and waiting are the miners and their opposition, suited executives.

THREE DAYS LATER, early Saturday morning. I am with Mike outside Hangar C at the Whitehorse Airport. Grey Mountain in the background has gotten a fresh covering of snow. We stand on the runway waiting for the fueling of the Cessna 402 Businessliner, converted to a flying ambulance. When we are inside and Mike is warming the engines, a cab pulls up to the plane bringing the nurse, twenty-eight-year-old Agnes Vanderkaauw. Soon we are airborne, heading to the small community of Mayo, 210 miles away. The problem is a childbirth with complications. Agnes, who came to the Yukon from Holland, is a veteran of Medevac calls. She sits back and reads a paperback novel as we head into the clouds.

Mike is recalling other Medevacs: childbirth emergencies, stabbings, shootings, and serious illnesses to which he has attended. "Some of them get complicated. Once I took a sick kid on with his old grandfather. After a few minutes the old guy leaned over and informed me the kid had infectious meningitis. Then after a few minutes I made contact with a lost American pilot trying to find Whitehorse. I had to talk him in. It was dark and cloudy and if all this isn't enough, a helicopter was taking a man to Whitehorse who had gone berserk. There were three guys holding the man down and the pilot had lost radio contact with Whitehorse. So I had to talk him and the other guy in while at the same time worrying about catching spinal meningitis."

An hour later we are landing on the gravel strip at Mayo. A couple of weather-beaten sheds in the snow and an old ambulance with faded maroon paint backing toward the plane. A sign on one of the sheds tells the story of the community on the other side of the woods.

MAYO

Yukon Territory

elevation 1659   180 miles from Arctic Circle

production of silver ore from

United Keno Mines

Mike and I help the driver load the lady on the stretcher into the plane while Agnes confers with the midwife. Then from the back of the ambulance like an afterthought appears the husband.

To myself I wonder of all the babies about to be born at this very moment all over the world, how many of them are struggling for life in such a desolate spot. Snow-covered hills and bare trees and an immense land dwarf this one little drama.

The woman's moans are punctuated by screams. As we get into the air Agnes calculates her contractions are three-and-a-half minutes apart. Mike flies the plane, Agnes tends to the woman, even I seem to have a function, that of observer or stretcher bearer. Only the husband has nothing to do. Nothing to do, that is, but sit in the back worrying with sad eyes and furrowed brow. He is a burly, rough, capable-looking guy but now is reduced to helplessness.

There is little conversation on the flight back through the overcast skies. The only sounds are the agonized moans that grow more frequent, the soothing words of the nurse, and the drone of the motors.

We reach the Klondike road and are over Lake Laberge ten minutes from the airport and the woman begins frantically tossing her head and screaming. There is the Alaska Highway now and the town is visible. Her face has gone deep red, her blond hair is wet and in tangles over the pillow. We are descending, the Vasis lights are switching from white to red and as the wheels set down, the woman screams violently like a sudden stab of a knife out of a darkened alleyway. The ambulance waits with swirling lights. We taxi toward it and it comes to meet us. Doors are opened and everything is a chaos of crouched-over, anxious activity. We load the stretcher onto the ambulance but the vehicle doesn't move. Agnes is inside hunched over the woman. There is a final loud scream and sobbing and then the cry of a baby. The husband stands on tiptoe over the huddled figures and stares transfixed at the wet, red, mottled child.

Then the ambulance doors close and it drives off, taillights glimmering in the snowy gray morning. Mike and I watch it move across the runway and he says, "You know, I forgot to get breakfast this morning. I'm starved. Let's go find us some bacon and eggs."

Very little good can be said of the White Pass Trail until foot traffic ended. . . and the railroad tracks. . . reached Lake Bennett. It was tortuous for man and beast, impassable at times and the scene of frequent battles over toll roads. Between 2,000 and 3,000 horses were killed. . . by starvation, abuse and overwork. Epidemics of spinal meningitis were common. Murders, suicides, robberies, con games . . . were the order of the day. The trail had little to recommend it.

ARCHIE SATTERFIELD, *Chilkoot Pass*

10

THE WHITE PASS and Yukon Route Railway played an immensely important role in keeping the Alaska Highway crews equipped and supplied. It was built back in the Gold Rush days through the White Pass, neighbor of the Chilkoot, both symbols of the Klondike trek. I decided to make the trip to Skagway and wrangled a ride in the caboose out of Whitehorse one snowy morning, aware that I was backtracking through history, and doing it backward, as it were. All the action had moved from the coast inward. It was an easy trip, the 110 miles to Skagway, enlivened by the German cook going to Lake Bennett who interrupted his songs and monologues only long enough to drink from a quart bottle of vodka. I sat in the twin-seat cupola with the engineer, Rick Burleigh, watching the scenery. The next day would prove more difficult, which was appropriate because I would be following the route of the stampeders.

I got off the train in the dark at Skagway and the customs officer was a young woman and after I told her I wasn't bringing anything illegal into the country, she asked me where I was headed.

"The Skagway Inn," I said.

"Come on, I'll give you a ride."

She switched off the lights and closed up the customs shed. She worked for half an hour or so twice a day, seeing off the morning train and greeting the evening one. She had come to Alaska from Tampa, Florida, and had no desire to go back.

The Skagway Inn is a big two-story wooden Victorian structure of the kind they didn't build over the pass in the Yukon. Perhaps it has something to do with heating costs, Skagway being warmer due to the Japanese Current. Yet they did build this kind of house in Dawson City where the temperature in the winter is liable to hold at sixty below for weeks at a time. But Dawson City was mostly built by Americans. Whatever the reason, it is Canada's loss because these examples of Northwest Nineties style are testaments to the anticipation of the Gold Rush, the homey kind of buildings where the stampeders took their last comfort before jumping off into the unknown.

Wide plank floors, big old-fashioned iron beds. "'Why, Captain Jack Crawford stayed in your room,' manager Jerry McNamara tells me."

"Really?"

"Well, there is, ah, reason to believe he did."

"If he didn't he should have."

Everyone I talk to in Skagway is a White Pass worker—a curious situation, it being a one-company town and that company being Canadian. Skagway, it is said, is the Yukon's saltwater port. Skagway came into being because of the farsightedness of old Captain William Moore. The Chilkoot Pass is more famous as a Gold Rush route although the White was to eclipse it with the coming of the railroad. The

Chilkoot climbers became the Yukon's territorial symbol and it was the Chilkoot's popularity that brought the White into prominence and bore the town of Skagway.

The aggressive, competitive Chilkat Indians had long used the pass to trade with the Sticks on the Yukon River. The Chilkats traded sea products to the docile Sticks for pelts. The first whites began coming to the area in the 1850s but none went over the pass until George Holt did it in 1874.

Five years later, three prospectors tried to go over but were turned back by the Chilkats. In 1880 a party of nineteen miners led by a California prospector named Edmund Bean and accompanied by a naval party armed with rifles, sidearms, and a Gatling gun managed to climb the pass.

Brigadier General Nelson Miles, stationed at Vancouver Barracks, Washington, had no authority to explore Alaska and the Yukon as a representative of the United States Government. In 1881, he had applied for appropriations to do just this but was turned down, as well as reminded where his influence lay. Nevertheless, the next year at his own expense he sent out a party to explore the area. The expedition was led by Lieutenant Frederick Schwatka and it penetrated Canada with neither the consent nor the knowledge of the Dominion's government.

Schwatka and his men went over the pass without interference from the Chilkats. Schwatka named it Perrier Pass in honor of the president of the French Geographical Society. He named Lake Lindeman for the secretary of the Bremen Geographical Society and Miles Canyon after his superior. Lake Bennett was named after a New York *Herald* newsman. When the Canadian Government found out about Schwatka's exploration they were incensed. The antipathy, however, was short-lived, for not only did the Canadian Government not change any of the names Schwatka had imposed on the landscape, they even named a lake after him.

The Americans changed the name of the pass back to Chilkoot. Better it should be named after Indians than Frenchmen. Besides, Indian names could be pronounced.

In 1886 gold was found at 40 Mile and traffic over the Chilkoot began to increase. In 1887 the Canadian Government sent a survey team led by William Ogilvie to ascertain the actual boundary between Alaska and the Yukon. When Ogilvie got to the North he employed three men who were to become famous later on their own.

At the coast he was met by a local oldtimer called Captain Moore. William Moore had been born in Germany and had run away to sea, eventually settling in America. He had been a tow-boat operator on the Mississippi, fought in the war with Mexico, and prospected throughout the North. He believed there was another pass through the mountains and convinced Ogilvie to let him look for it. Moore took with him a white man who lived on the Salmon River in a log cabin furnished with a pump organ and filled with scientific treatises and books of philosophy. His name was

George Washington Carmack. Carmack was married to an Indian named Kate. She had a brother whom Carmack took along with him. He was called Skookum (strong man) Jim.

It didn't take long for Moore to find the pass, which he named White Pass, through the mountains. He was convinced there was going to be a gold rush. People ignored his ideas. In 1894 gold was discovered at Circle City. Moore had already cut a trail over White Pass and was even going around promoting a scheme for a railroad through the pass and now he was no longer ignored. He was considered crazy.

Moore made his home at the foot of his pass and built a sawmill and a wharf in anticipation of the rush to come. He called the settlement, quite naturally, Mooresville. In 1895 he helped the first stampeders, a party of Californian prospectors with tons of gear, over the White Pass.

Meanwhile the town of Dyea (pronounced Die-ee) was beginning to grow at the foot of Chilkoot Pass. Dyea had begun as the site of a Healy and Wilson trading post, two saloons, and a couple of cabins. A few years later when Carmack with Skookum Jim and Tagish Charlie discovered gold on Rabbit Creek, Moore's inevitable rush began. Dyea boomed and the overflow crowded Mooresville. The stampeders had little respect for Captain Moore. They changed the name of his settlement to Skaugway, which is Tlingit for "home of the north wind," and the word was corrupted to Skagway. The new city's fathers ran Main Street right through Moore's cabin and when Soapy Smith arrived, his men virtually ran the captain out of town.

Samuel B. Steele of the NWMP, known as the Lion of the Yukon, called Skagway "little better than a hell on earth."

Soapy Smith, who earned his sobriquet by selling bars of soap wrapped in five-dollar bills on the downtown streets of western American cities, ruled Skagway and devoted his time and that of his gang to separating the stampeders from their money. His dance-hall girls took their share, his Sixth Avenue gambling dens prospered, and his street-corner three-card monte men added to the coffers.

The more upright stampeders were swindled at Soapy's real-estate offices or rolled at his "Information Centers." He even had employees, called "sure-fire men," plying their trade on the trails. His cappers worked the passes steering cheechakos to the sure-fire men and their crooked campfire card games.

Chilkoot Pass became so crowded that stampeders began to use Moore's White Pass, which was easier although seven miles longer. In 1898 three Victoria, British Columbia, businessmen obtained a charter from the Canadian Government to build a railroad through the pass. When they were unable to obtain financial backing they sold the charter to the Close Brothers of London and construction by the company of Michael J. Heney began on May 27, 1898.

Two days later the ice broke on Lake Bennett and the stampeders who had come over the passes and camped for the winter began the float to Dawson. The shores of the lake had been crowded with tents, shacks, and sawmills. The spruce trees around the lake had been depleted for boat wood. On May 30, the day after break-up, 30,000 men and women left Lake Bennett in 7,124 boats.

Railroad track reached the summit of White Pass in February 1899, and Bennett on July 6, 1899. On July 29, a year later, crews heading south from Whitehorse met those going north from Bennett at the community of Carcross. The completion of the railroad spelled the end for Dyea. The Chilkoot was no longer needed. In a last-moment desperate act the town of Dyea petitioned the United States Government to donate the entire inlet to Canada so that the Dominion might have a seaport and Dyea might survive. The post office finally closed in 1902.

After the Gold Rush the population of Skagway fell from fifteen thousand to five hundred, where it remained until the building of the Alaska Highway. After the war it leveled at its present population of nine hundred, nearly all employed by White Pass, which brings materials to Skagway via its boats, ships them over the pass on its trains to Whitehorse, where they are met by its trucks.

At night Skagway's Broadway is deserted save for one pickup parked in a mud puddle and dark but for the warm glow of light coming from the Igloo Bar. On these winter nights there are no reminders of Captain Moore or Soapy Smith, but come June and the tourist season their ghosts will rise again.

In the morning I have breakfast with a ship's engineer and his crewmate, an ordinary seaman. They are bound for San Francisco and the younger guy is pleased; he doesn't like the work and anyway he has a girlfriend on Stinson Beach. Around us are White Pass construction workers and the waitress is married to one of the train engineers. After eating I grab my duffel and walk down to the depot along the board sidewalks. It is still dark at nine o'clock and a wet snow is falling. Up on the mountain a blue electric star glows to indicate the pass.

I was the only passenger. I sat in the caboose next to the kerosene-burning stove. It was cozy during the slow climb up the hill. My feet, which were near the stove, were warm but the rest of me wasn't. I huddled in my parka. There was the smell of the kerosene and the cracked worn leather covering the chairs. The caboose must date back decades. The insides are wooden like an old cottage and there is a porch out the back and a lantern over the door. I considered giving an election speech when we got to Cannacks.

It took three hours to negotiate the twisting nineteen-mile uphill route to Dead Horse Gulch, named after the three thousand pack animals that died during the summer of '98. At White Horse summit, the British Columbia boundary, I looked out across the mountains to where the old trail is covered with snow and I thought of Robert Service making this same train ride in 1904 and glancing down from this same point and writing in his journal, "I was glad I had not been one of those grim stalwarts of the Great Stampede."

It took until three in the afternoon to get to Lake Bennett where there was a lunch stop and a crew change. The crew ate in a long dining hall around a wooden table creaking under the weight of a turkey and a roast of beef, proving the cook was not to be deterred by a hangover. The women wheeled in trays of vegetables, fruits, salads, and one devoted to desserts: cakes, homemade pies, and puddings. Rick Burleigh was there helping himself.

After lunch I saw a guy sitting in the lobby reading a John Le Carré novel. His name was John Webb, he teaches school in Whitehorse, and he was going to Skagway and Juneau to spend part of his Christmas vacation. We took a walk around the area while the crew made a repair on the train. High on the hill overlooking the lake sits the shell of the old Presbyterian church, the only reminder of the Gold Rush.

The train didn't get five miles before one of the cars derailed. This necessitated a two-hour wait for the crane car to come from the Bennett siding. After we got started I sat with Rick up in the cupola. We talked and looked straight ahead at the snow falling and covering any sign of the steel rails. There was a sheer mountain wall to our right and a panorama of rugged wilderness to our left.

Rick allowed as how the Americans were to blame for the derailment. He ran his hand across the sooty wall and studied his smudged fingers. "Ah, to them it's just a job. They don't care. We clean the cars and they dirty them. But then, maybe I'm a fanatic."

He told me he had always wanted to work on trains. "My father was a yard clerk with the Canadian Pacific and my granddaddy was a CPR brakeman. I have my brakeman's and conductor's license as well as my engineer's. I began with the CPR seventeen years ago down in Vancouver when I was nineteen. I quit a couple of times and tried other things. I drove a truck for a time. But I kept coming back to railroading. Came up to the Yukon eight years ago. Smartest thing I ever did."

He stroked his beard, looked straight ahead, and smiled. "Yeah, I love the old railroad. You see that old steam engine sitting back there in Bennett? Well, I'm trying to convince the company to purchase it and restore it. I'm willing to do the work just to get it running. It would pay for itself in one tourist season. Make a million dollars, people coming to ride on an oldtime train. We ought to get it before the Americans do anyway."

We stopped at Carcross, named for the caribou herds that used to pass this way, and took on a couple of surveyors going to Whitehorse. Two miles out of Carcross where the double line of tracks merge, we came to a stop as Rick's walkie-talkie started bleeping. He conferred with the engineer and then the dispatcher. It seemed like there had been a mix-up and we would have to wait where we were on the double tracks because another train was coming from Whitehorse on the single track. "We'll be here another couple of hours," said Rick.

I borrowed a pair of snowshoes from one of the surveyors and made my way back to Carcross. It is now a cluster of trailers and small homes around the three main buildings: the rail depot, the Caribou Hotel, and Matthew Watson's General Store. The Tutshi sternwheeler is pulled up onshore beside the depot. Carcross, until the Gold Rush, was an occasional Tagish Indian village. Here the shallow sluggish streams empty Lake Bennett into Tagish Lake and provide good fishing.

George Carmack, Tagish Charlie, and Skookum Jim are all buried in the little cemetery at Carcross. Tagish Charlie used to own the Caribou Hotel where I went in to get a coffee and a sandwich. Two Indian women are drinking beer in the lounge and in the dining room a little Indian girl is sitting at the counter eating a bag of potato chips and ignoring the color television and the parrot in the adjacent cage.

The parrot, though, successor to the famous Polly, is devoting all her attention to the television. There is a CBC show being broadcast from Toronto. One man is interviewing another and the nameless bird had taken exception to the interviewee's high-pitched voice. Whenever he speaks, the bird drowns him out with terrific squawks. He is a beautiful yellow, red, green, and blue bird but his predecessor, although more scraggly, was a legend.

Polly arrived during the Gold Rush and was bought by a Captain Alexander from a broke and disgruntled miner returning home. Alexander made a little money from his own mining operation and was going Outside on a vacation with his wife. He left Polly at the Caribou for safekeeping. The captain and his wife were killed when their ship, the *Sophia*, foundered between Skagway and Juneau. Polly stayed on at the Caribou. It liked to drink and the patrons, of course, encouraged the bird. It would drink until it fell off its perch and lay on the bottom of the cage with its feet in the air.

One day in the late fifties, Polly suddenly stopped talking to adults except when they would ask him or her—its sex was never determined—whether it wanted a cracker. To which the bird would reply, "Go to hell." From then on Polly talked only to children, engaging them in long, serious conversations and answering their questions with what may have seemed like gibberish to adults but evidently made sense to the Indian kids.

Polly lived on until one day in 1972 when it was found at the bottom of its cage, feet up, not drunk, but finally dead. Polly was buried in the cemetery near Skookum Jim, Tagish Charlie, and George Washington Carmack. The burial ceremony was hosted by a well-known local guide Johnny Johns who sang "I Love You Truly" while accompanying himself on the skin drum.

Finally the train from Whitehorse passed us and we got moving. We climbed the Watson Valley, picked up a little speed going down the other side, reaching Whitehorse at nine in the evening. There were no Gold Rushers getting off to catch the sternwheeler to Dawson, no bookish bank clerks scribbling verse, no soldiers to meet the train. There was a turbine motor, though, for an electrical plant and two flatcars loaded with truck trailers. The Yukon is poised on the verge of provincial status, pipeline, and boom time. That old narrow-gauge train had hauled a lot of history and, I have a feeling, it is going to again.

To look up or down no road
but it stretches and waits for you,
however long but it stretches
and waits for you.

WALT WHITMAN, "Song of the Open Road"

L EAVING WHITEHORSE HEADING for the U.S. border. The snow is blowing across the Alaska Highway and the windshield wipers thud out their steady rubber/metal beat. The low hills on either side of the highway climb gradually to the mountains and the route leads arrow-straight into the white horizon.

Wayne King hunkers forward, his forearms resting across the big wheel, a lock of blond hair falling in his face. He doesn't say much but when he does it is direct and to the point. He is six feet tall, dark complexioned, wears boots, jeans, flannel western shirt, and a sleeveless, down-filled vest. He is handsome, so much so that all the young waitresses blush when he comes in the cafés. The older ones hover around, wanting to mother him. He reminds me of Gary Cooper and if his hair were curly he might resemble a profile on a Greek coin. But no, he is too western, too much a northern mountain man, to call ancient Greeks to mind; except that being sparing of speech, Wayne might be deemed laconic, from *lakonikos*, which was used to describe the Spartans.

And Spartan is the interior of this Kluane Freight Lines semi cab in which we're riding. No pin-ups, knickknacks, or doodads. Your basic truck with room only for necessities, like the CB radio. In the bed at our backs we've stored our parkas on top of which Wayne has rested his opened attaché case with the bills of lading.

Wayne was born and raised in the Yukon. His father came to the territory thirty years ago and drove trucks all over the North. After high school Wayne, who is twenty-five but seems older because of his quiet self-assurance, worked construction jobs, lived at home, and saved his money. Two years ago he and his father started Kluane Freight Lines.

Wayne had agreed to take me along to the Alaska border in exchange for giving him a hand with his deliveries along the way. I wanted to look at the highway from a different perspective. He fetched me from my hotel in his pick-up truck and we drove to the industrial park area at the edge of Whitehorse; where the semi was waiting on a snow-covered lot.

His father had backed a five-ton up to the side trailer door. We got out of the pick-up and loaded the rest of the mail and freight onto the truck. I hoisted my duffel bag up onto the trailer, we locked her up and took off, lumbering out of the yards past corrugated tin sheds and cinder-block garages and out to Two Mile Hill and the highway.

He makes the run to Beaver Creek at the border twice a week, Tuesday and Friday, a day each way.

"The one who's not driving stays back doing the office work or repairs."

I asked him if they had plans to expand operations.

"Nope. Got enough to do now. We did buy the second tractor this year. just want to make a decent living. We work seven days a week to do it. Reckon we'll have to hire a part-time man next summer."

"What? You mean you don't pull up at every truck stop to play country songs on the jukebox and flirt with the waitresses and then pop those little red pills to make up for the time you lost?"

He grins. "Maybe I wish I did but I got to work too hard. You'll see."

We picked up a brand-new fifteen-mile section of the highway past Yukon Crossing where the stagecoaches on the old Dawson–Whitehorse road were ferried across the Takhini River.

Our first stop is at Champagne, an Indian encampment on the highway; a cluster of houses and sheds. The people here trap in the winter and guide hunters and fishermen in the summer and fall. Champagne used to be the end of the trail that Jack Dalton had blazed from Haines, Alaska, to the Yukon River in 1902. Dalton established a series of trading posts along his route, rented horses, and charged travelers a hefty toll. He got filthy rich even if his mercenary ways didn't earn him a plethora of friends.

We stop only long enough to hand a canvas sack of mail to an Indian woman who appears from behind a bearskin hanging in her doorway.

A half a mile down the road is the Indian burial ground with a little house built over each grave. The ancient customs hold that the spirit might return and if so it should be sheltered and provided with cached items for its comfort. A sign at the gate advises:

THIS IS NOT A TOURIST SIGHT. RESPECT
OUR PRIVATE PROPERTY AS WE RESPECT YOURS.

Twenty miles farther on is the Aishihik River and the road to Otter Falls, an engraving of which found its way to the back of the Canadian five-dollar bill.

A few miles later we pass a pick-up truck pulling a trailer in the other direction. "Pilgrims," says Wayne. They were the only tourists we would see the entire three hundred miles to the border.

"The road is easier to drive in the winter. The snow makes it smoother. The dust can be a nuisance, but the real problem is those pilgrims. They do funny things, like you will be driving around a curve and practically in the middle of the road is one of them taking a picture of something."

Near Pine Lake we see a pick-up truck overturned on the road apron.

"Must have been icy last night," Wayne comments matter-of-factly.

I try to get him to expound more on tourists.

"The scariest thing that ever happened with one of them was on the other side of Kluane. I came over a hill and there at the bottom was a station wagon stopped dead in the middle of the road. The man driving the car had his window opened a crack and he was feeding this little bear that had come out onto the road. I had to hit the brakes hard and I came to a stop not a foot away from the car. The man gave me a dirty look 'cause the bear ran back into the woods. I let him know I wasn't very pleased that I almost killed his family and myself."

"THE GREAT MOUNTAINS, wherein sublimity so much excels our daily things, that in their presence experience dissolves, and we seem to enter a kind of eternity."

Hilaire Belloc said it, and coming over the rise and down into the Shakwa Valley you see for the first time the Auriol Range of the endless St. Elias system with the highway town of Haines Junction nothing more than a few specks on the hem of its snow-white bridal train. If a Cinerama camera topped the same rise it would be with Wagnerian accompaniment, but in real life silence is appropriate because before the panorama of mountains folding in upon themselves—dissolving into one another in a ragged series of ridges working upward from the vast glaciers, the far-flung ice fields, a great gray granite world played upon by icy fingers and volcanoes gushing snow and candle wax—one can only feel the hush of awe. The range stretches far into the distance, hundreds of peaks disappear truly as if into eternity. No one has named the peaks, no one has even seen them in their entirety; there are unimagined worlds beyond the first mountain walls and hidden tarns where mountain sheep have come to drink for thousands of years.

We go about our woebegone human experience against this splendid alpine background. We call at the general store and the Yukon Territorial Government work camp where we unload lumber and then to the log cabin post office with its roof of snow. There is an entire living room set in the back of the truck covered with heavy black plastic sheeting and we have to deliver it to a house in Haines Junction. We turn down the road indicated on the instructions and all of a sudden there in the midst of the dense forest ringed round by Canada's highest mountains is a desperate, hopeful clutch of suburbia. Ten homes that could be ten miles from Detroit. A couple of ranch houses. Some split levels.

A man with a beard comes from one of the houses and waves to us. Wayne backs as close to the house as possible and we put on our coats and get out of the truck. The three of us troop through the snow carrying the stuff into the house. Wayne lugs a chair and the man and I take either end of the couch. As we go through the front door I see the wife peeking out from the living room archway to see her new furniture. There is applause coming from the color television as a couple win a prize of some kind. Everything is put in the basement, which is half converted into a rec room. Wayne presents the bill to the husband who studies it with furrowed concentration and solemnly writes a check while his wife takes a kitchen knife to the plastic to make sure the living room set is the proper color. Her expression is one of excitement mingled with self-satisfaction. The husband hands over the check and sighs resignedly. She puts her arms around his waist and we leave.

We stop a few miles down the highway for a break at the MacIntosh Lodge. A three-legged German shepherd stands before the door watching us approach and wagging its tail. Inside is a crew of YTG workers having coffee. They all nod at Wayne and say hello but they stay quiet. I realize it is on my account; not unfriendliness but a typical Yukon reserve. They just don't know who I am. The waitress brings coffee. I have been studying the menu and I ask, "What's 'Surprise Soup'?"

"I can't tell you." She smiles. "It's a surprise."

"Well, I think I know what it might be. I saw that dog out there's missing a leg."

She laughs and the men laugh. I've broken the ice. I must then be a regular guy and not some kind of company or government inspector.

"Say, Wayne, there's a YFL truck overturned at Mile 1031. You know who it might be?"

"Sure don't, Les. Not this time of week."

"Looks bad."

"Yep. You fellows keeping busy?"

"Too busy. We're hauling all day for the paving job."

The project has begun to pave the Haines Highway from Alaska to Haines Junction in the spring. The second stage of the plan supposedly is to pave the Alaska Highway from Haines Junction to the border. After we leave the lodge and are on our way I say to Wayne, "I think it's a shame they're going to pave the road."

"Why's that?"

"It's going to change everything. The Yukon will be different. I guess that's a romantic view but that's how I feel, that it's a bad thing."

Wayne shrugged, thought it over, and said, "Well, it'll sure make my job easier. It'll be good for the territory too. More tourists will stop. More business will get done. Politicians feel we're not likely to get provincial status if our only highway is unpaved."

"Yeah, true enough, but still…"

Wayne has his view and as a Yukoner, a man whose work is dependent on the road, he is absolutely right so I don't worry the point out loud. The road will get paved of course and the Yukon will become a province but it won't be the same anymore. The words themselves tell the story succinctly enough. It is precisely the difference between a province and a territory. Whose imagination was ever stirred by the word "province"; but "territory" conjures an image of unexplored, untamed land, the image of a frontier. Romantic? Sure but romance is the currency of the Yukon. Always has been. It is nice to have been there before they paved the road. In years to come I will be able to say, "I was up in this country years before they ever paved the old Alcan. It was different then."

Kluane Park headquarters looks deserted, a lone red light glowing in one of the buildings. The peaks of the St. Elias Range are lost in cloud and fog. One of them is elusive Mount Logan, at 19,860 feet the tallest peak in Canada. More impressive even than its height is its sheer massive bulk, rising 13,100 feet out of the Stewart Glacier, its summit ridge, one of the longest in the world, at just under fifteen miles. It is this mass and Mount Logan's isolated position, surrounded as it is, protected, by other towering peaks like Mount King at 17,000 feet and Mount Kennedy at 14,000 feet that has always made it seem indomitable. Because it can rarely even be seen and only from certain points in the Yukon, Mount Logan remains shrouded in fog and mystery.

We pass the Jarvis River, Sulphur Lake, and Christmas Creek, so named by a Presbyterian minister who discovered gold here in 1903. A mile farther on, just past Boutillier's Summit, Kluane Lake comes into view for the first time. Then for a few miles the highway follows the old wagon road from Whitehorse to the Kluane gold fields. Its terminus was Silver City at the southern end of the lake. All that remains now of this settlement that was occupied until 1925 are deserted cabins, some of them furnished with wire cages, which represent a mink-ranching venture—Silver City's desperate experiment to stay alive after the gold disappeared. In front of the old trading post the rusted roof of a Model T Ford pokes from the drifted snow.

A side road leads to the lake and the scattered buildings of the Arctic Institute. A man leaves his log cabin laboratory to come fetch the mail. A single-engine plane sits with iced propeller blade on the rough gravel runway. The wind swoops down across the jade water of Kluane Lake, shattering the thin film of ice at the middle.

A mile or so beyond Slim's River, the original pioneer road can be seen winding up the hillside, the top of which is called Soldiers' Summit. There the official Alcan opening ceremony was held on November 20, 1942. Just north of the summit is a cross that can be seen from the highway. This marks the burial spot of Alex Fisher, a well-loved local prospector and trapper whose cabin was nearby. Fisher died in 1941 and was buried on the lake shore near his cabin. Unfortunately in 1942, the Army surveyors determined that the highway had to go right through his cabin and his grave. Despite the protests of local people, his remains were moved to its present site. Up until the sixties the bus driver would always stop and show passengers the grave and tell the story of this self-reliant pioneer.

At Destruction Bay we leave several sacks of mail at the post office and drop off twenty cases of Coke at the highway service station and restaurant. Then we spend half an hour unloading food and supplies at a work camp in the bush near the lake. People at Destruction Bay have lately begun to promote the legend that their settlement was named for the terrible winds that would capsize boats full of Gold Rushers, sending dozens to watery graves; but the actual, if more prosaic, origin of the name goes back to the war when one day a high wind knocked down several Army tents on the shore.

In a few more miles we come upon the closed-down Burwash Lodge where I had stayed before. We turn and pass the lodge, following a road that links the lake with Indian cabins on either side, a medical trailer, and a post office. We take the mail in and Indians and half-breeds are milling about; there's hardly elbow room, a couple of dogs creep between boots and legs. Behind the counter are empty letter slots gathering dust. In the back are a pot-bellied wood stove and shelves of canned goods.

As we pull away I say to Wayne, "It looks like the post office is the social center of Burwash."

"Sure," he replies. "Everyone waits there for their government checks."

We stop at a lodge on a hillside overlooking Kluane Lake. From our table by the window we can see the dark, jagged tops of trees descending the hill to the lake, which is still and smooth like a sheet of dark glass in the early evening. The man and woman who operate the lodge are sitting at another table having coffee. They are friendly and happy to have company. "Who's your friend?" they ask Wayne.

The daughter serves the coffee and brings homemade apple cake. The husband complains about the furnace, which keeps breaking down every few hours. They talk about their son, who has gone Outside to college. I can remember pulling into the place for gas when the kid was barely able to wrestle the hose from the pump.

When we've finished they walk us to the door and say good-bye, resisting our attempts to pay for the cake and coffee.

We stop at Mountain View Lodge, a little place in the valley with a gas pump, garage, and log home. A long-haired guy with a beard comes out followed by two husky dogs. He is minding the business while the owners are vacationing in the Philippines. They're due back that night and he is excited because he can leave for Whitehorse the next day. He's been there alone for three weeks. "'Bout to go crazy," he declares. He hasn't seen anyone since Wayne stopped on his return trip two days earlier.

There is a litter of Malamute pups to greet us at the Koidern Lodge. Inside, the heat isn't working and a woman in sweaters sits around the fire with two men, one is half Indian, and his features are fine and aristocratic. He looks like a northern

Italian count but for his swollen and cracked hands folded around a cup of coffee.

We pull into the White River Lodge five miles along the other side of the highway. I know from other summer trips that this is a busy spot. They rent cabins and horses, guide hunters, sell groceries and liquor, and do towing, welding, and vehicle repairs; but now in the winter it is quiet, desolate in the snow. Inside the operators and their sons and daughters sit around the tables reading Harlequin romances and Robert Ruark novels. One girl drums her fingers on the table top and stares out at the softly falling snow. There is a young man there from Vancouver who gave up on the city life three years ago and came North. He stopped in the White River Lodge and volunteered to do whatever needed to be done. The family took him on and he's stayed learning the ways of the northern outdoors.

In one corner of the room, pinned to the wall and piled on a table are postcards, bumper stickers, plaques, cups and glasses, plaster statuettes—summer souvenirs gathering dust.

After we leave I mention to Wayne that they look a trifle bored.

"Nope." He is quick to disagree. "They don't mind sitting around like that. They got plenty to do in the summer. They keep busy now too, running a trapline the other side of the road back in the woods."

It is thirty more miles to Beaver Creek and Canadian customs. The road narrows through the heavy forest. It is dark and the snow-laden branches of trees glitter in the headlights of the big Mack truck.

We go through customs with a salute, unload supplies at the two service stations, and pull up in front of the post office. We have several sacks of mail to carry off and cases of food for the adjoining restaurant. We unload with the help of a middle-aged Indian with a duck-tail haircut who is wearing Old Spice aftershave lotion. It takes us another hour to make deliveries in the residential area of Beaver Creek. Boxes of food at a couple of trailers, a twenty-foot length of quarter-inch plywood to a man who is building a boat in his basement, and a waterbed to a giggling couple in a modern ranch house. Finally we're done. The day is over.

We're cold and tired and there is warm food and cold beer waiting. The tiny bar at the lodge is filled with truck drivers and Beaver Creek locals out for a loud old time on a Friday night. The television plays on in the background. People are shooting pool over in a corner. Men match coins for beers at the bar. The portly cigar-smoking bartender stands Wayne and me a couple of rounds.

The beer flows, everyone at the bar in turn buys a round of beer for the bar. Shouted conversations are held, men you will never see again are true friends for a couple of hours. People make bets on football games being played four thousand miles away, mouthing names more exotic than Jeddah and Timbuktu: Alabama and Penn State.

There is talk of traplines and big moose kills, how to fix frozen-up motors, how to get a trailer back into the bush. The bartender passes around some calendars for the new year. One old Italian fellow studies the calendar with the Old Spice-scented Indian. The Indian points his brown finger to the first of January. "New moon," he says and then several squares along taps the page: "Full moon. Going to be sixty below that week for sure."

The night rolls on. The crowd thins. Wayne goes out to the truck to sleep. I have another beer and rent a cabin for the night.

In the morning I have a big breakfast of bacon and eggs to get me on my way. Wayne and I make promises to look for each other in the bars of Whitehorse sometime in the future. At a nearby table the owner of the place, a sixty-year-old with a white crew cut, is haggling with a young White Pass truck driver about unions and wages.

"You fellows got it too soft. All that money and can't make a move lessen the company tells you. Why, I used to drive up here from Spokane in the old days, making a buck-twenty-five an hour."

He's a crotchety character in a T-shirt with scrawny arms and faded, wrinkled tattoos.

The Canadian driver laughs. "When was that, Dad? The Depression?"

"Hell it was! Late fifties."

"You were *had*."

"Weren't neither. Whatta you know about it, anyway?"

To me the old guy says, "You going to Alaska you better get moving unless you plan to sit around here all day!"

That is as good as any cue to get going. I thank Wayne for the ride and say good-bye. He ambles off and hoists himself up into the cab for the run back to Whitehorse.

It is pitch-black at eight in the morning and cold, which is the way it should be on the Alcan. I pull my parka close around me, grab my duffel, and feel the fresh snow under my boots. I've covered the wildest part now, in a couple of miles the pavement and Alaska begin. Down the road the lights of Far West Texaco are glowing in the dark and America is just over that ridge. Maybe one of the Alaska trucks will give me a ride and I'll have my next beer, make it a Bud, tonight in a club on Second Avenue and a fitting reward it will be too, after all these miles. So I set off walking toward the lights, feeling crazily elated despite the dark, the snow, the cold, right down the middle of that deserted road.

12

THERE I WAS just a moment, and nearly forty years ago, walking down that cold, black night Alcan road. I wore the romance and possibility of that land wrapped around me, snug in them like my parka. I vowed to return, and did and have many times over the decades. So many trips have I made since, so many experiences and memories and images have I accumulated, that the notion of it all, my time in the far North, seems like a mandala or one of those old cardboard-tube kaleidoscopes.

One little twist and there I am in Dawson City in the winter waiting out the ice and snow, a long wait, until break-up, sitting by the oil barrel stove in a little house by the Yukon River, Half of me warm, the other half certainly not.

Me working for Yukon White Pass Route in Dawson, unloading planes, shifting boxes to another, smaller, plane bound for the settlement of Old Crow and loading the rest onto a truck for delivery in town.

Sitting at a campfire with a couple of friends somewhere near the Dempster Highway, the outline of the Blackstone mountains still visible in the night sky. We went up to the Arctic Circle and beyond all the way to Inuvik, NWT, which was then the end of the road but as of August, 2018 the summer road has been pushed through to Tuktoyuktok on the Arctic Ocean.

On December 7, 1991 I set off once more for the Alcan territory. It was the fiftieth anniversary of the bombing of Pearl Harbor which seemed appropriate because that event had emphasized the need for the road.

In Dawson Creek, mile zero, I walked around town, stopped in a few shops and called at a pub where I immediately fell into conversation with a long, lean, seventy-year-old truck driver named Gene Wilkinson who was still working and who informed me he'd come out from Ontario during the original construction period.

He'd been awed then and remained awed by the ferocious beauty of the place. Wilkinson allowed as how it brought out his poetic nature that he usually kept hidden way down deep. "I wrote poems about it then, and still do."

He took out a folded piece of paper from his wallet and began to recite the pencilled words written upon it.

The gears they growled and the motor barked
As I steadily gave her the gun
Up the heavy drag on the other side
On toward the setting sun.

At the top of one hundred and forty-three
Was a scene of joy to behold

The trees below like thistles
And the mountains tinged with gold.

It was forty degrees below zero on the bus to Whitehorse when the heater broke down. When we got off for rest stops it actually seemed less cold outside.

There was a young Australian fellow across the aisle who complained about what he considered the bleak landscape outside the windows. At one point he exclaimed, "How can anybody live here?!"

"Just wait," I told him.

His complaining ended about the time we got to Summit Lake as the road began to twist and dip and rise. At Toad River when the bus pulled up to the lodge, he got out, looked around and said to me, "All right, all right. I can see why people live here."

In Whitehorse I was fortunate to meet John Kastelnick who used to be an Indian agent in the Northwest Territories covering his immense territory by dogsled. Now he was a liaison between businesses and the Yukon Tourism Department. After a few hours in his company I found John to be a perfect transitional figure for the Yukon and Alaska Highway territory. He had all the old skills but none of the rough edges so he was able to negotiate a relatively smooth passage in the North. He offered to drive me to the end of the road at Fairbanks.

The landscape was as spectacular as ever even if the occasional settlements showed signs of the contemporary world's encroachment.

As we wound our way north and west, I noticed now and again a lone Indian trudging through the snow by the side of the road. It occurred to me that the road was built without permission or consultation with the people who had lived on it forever.

The little town of Haines Junction at the entrance to Kluane National Park resembled confetti on a snow-white bridal train. The mountains look brutal in December but in the months of sunshine the peaks burst like gray fingers through icing sugar. Then the meadows are alive with delicate blue Jacob's ladder and magenta fireweed.

We cross the border and spend the night in Tok, Alaska, at the junction of the Alcan and Richardson Highways.

Alaska may have once been called 'where the highway begins' after the rough, dirt-and-gravel Canadian stretch but now that asphalt is not maintained and everything along the road seems a victim of desuetude and decrepitude. Alaska, post-pipeline boom, had the feel of a third-world country.

Fairbanks put me in mind of a frigid and abandoned Guatemala City.

The only business open on Second Avenue, Fairbanks' once jumping main stem, is a combination grocery-liquor store. The clerk is suspicious behind his iron grate until I comment on his handgun, the butt of which is sticking out of his waistband.

"A .38," he says. "Your .357 Magnum's for cowboys. Too much gun. I ain't shooting elephants. Twenty-two bounces. Thirty-eight's just the thing for shooting humans."

I'm told that the only time there is activity out on the street is the day welfare checks are issued. Then the bars do a decent business and on the sidewalks you see passed-out drunks, tired old prostitutes and young adolescent prostitutes; there are fist fights between Indians and Inuit as white crackheads watch before falling out.

It is not with reluctance that we leave the once Number One All-American city.

There were other trips, especially a 2001 journey from North Vancouver on the Royal Hudson train to Prince George and on to Whitehorse by bus.

It was on that trip crossing the Tetsa River north of Fort Nelson that I became acquainted with a young guy named Arthur who described himself as being 'half-Indian, half Russian.'

The first thing he said to me was, "Watch when we go around this bend. A beautiful view of Steamboat Mountain.

"The old Indians called it that because it reminded them of the white man's steamboats. And the whites named the next big mountain Indian Head."

I remembered that the first time I saw a wolf in the wild it was from a bus window like this one and it was loping along with Steamboat Mountain as a background.

"I wish I could paint that," said the voice in back of me.

Turning all the way I around I saw a guy who didn't look like most people's idea of an artist, unless it was Anthony Quinn playing Gauguin.

He had a wide mouth, broken nose, black eyes and a crescent scar on his forehead. A young Indian Quinn after a bar fight. He admitted having gotten interested in art while doing a stint in prison.

"There was an old Indian in there, a carver. He was real calm in the middle of all the noise and hassles in the joint. That impressed me, his stillness. I asked if I could watch him work and he let me. I watched him for months before I ever dared to touch a piece of wood."

Arthur was going home from Terrace, B.C. after losing his two-year-old truck in a wager on a boxing match.

He told me a story about being in a camp for geologists at Burwash where he was a handyman and got to stay in one of the cabins.

He told stories about the camp and the characters and like all good storytellers he worked in interesting digressions. One was about a grizzly bear who closed in on him but turned away at the last moment. "Some tourists shot the bear. I sawed off the hands at the wrists. I wanted the claws for a mask. I put the hands in a pot to boil on the stove but my dog somehow got them out and hid them."

Arthur took a nearly full pint bottle of vodka from his coat and handed it to me. I poured a shot or two into my take-out coffee cup but he put some more in there, saying, "No, no. We're partners now. We have to share everything equally."

Then there was another camp story about coming home early one afternoon and finding his girlfriend in bed with another camp worker. "When the guy saw me he looked terrified, jumped out of bed and started pulling his clothes on. He'd heard stories about me. He ran out."

"What did you do?" I asked.

"Just stood there for a second, then I left and went to the pub. I had a couple of drinks and when I got back to the cabin it was all cleaned up, beds made, dishes washed. She done the laundry too, and there was all my stuff, ironed and in piles. Shirts here, pants there, underwear.

"So I transferred all those neat piles into my suitcase and left, never said a word to her. I drove all the way to Terrace."

Arthur had spent half his life in institutions. "Sometimes I even done the deed but other times I was innocent."

Earlier in the trip, I had talked to a Korean guy who wanted me to get off the bus at Watson Lake and help him with a scheme he had to make a lot of money.

At Liard River, the Korean and I started talking again.

"You sure you not get off?" He tugged at the sleeve of my parka. "Make plenty money."

"I'm positive, Jack."

"Jack! Hah, hah, hah!"

Arthur warned me not to trust him. "These Chinese guys, they have these gangs, you know. Tongs or something."

Arthur told a story about going over to Alaska to try and sell his art. He got hassled in a bar by two Inuit brothers. "Real mean guys. They're a mixed-up people, you know, Eskimos. Many of them are inbred. Well, these two started ranking me for being Indian. Then it's 'what the fuck you doing in our country?'" He told them again he was just in Alaska to sell his art and didn't want any trouble. Then they grabbed him and started hitting.

"So I reached down and grabbed the blade from my boot and stabbed one of them. The other one starts hollering about what I'd done."

Arthur got out of there, started the truck and took off.

After crossing over into the Yukon, soon Arthur was talking about the problems of being in prison but also the hardships of being 'free.'

He didn't really complain, though, nor did he recite any litany of woes, particularly those that might befall a young, scary-looking Indian male.

Reaching into his overcoat pocket, Arthur came up with a thick packet of aluminum foil such as might contain a sandwich.

He unfolded the foil. It wasn't a sandwich. "What do you think this looks like?"

"It looks, to tell you the truth, like a hunk of flesh with brown hairs sticking out of it. Hell, it looks like a scalp."

Arthur let loose with a yelp, followed by a loud burst of laughter. I caught the bus driver's glance in the big rearview mirror.

"Well, yes, indeed, it does. Doesn't it!"

Arthur was in Prince George with a few days to wait for this bus to the Yukon. One night he went into a bar and spotted 'some savages from home.'

They were sitting with two white guys.

"One of the whites was good people. But the other was truculent from the beginning."

This one started digging at Arthur.

"Everyone tried to ignore him. The other white fellow even advised him to shut up. But the guy continued to stick little barbs in, all of them directed at me. Finally, I just asked him, 'What's bothering you, man?'

"He kept quiet for a few minutes then started again. I told him to cool it. He said, 'Oh, yeah? And if I don't what are you going to do, scalp me?'

"He kept on like that. 'You going to scalp me, Chief? You going on the war path?' The others were embarrassed. But then when he got in my face with, 'Yeah, just try and scalp me,' I went, 'Okay, I will.'" As he said that, his hand went into his overcoat pocket again and this time was holding a hunting knife.

His eyes flashed as he told the story and his look hardened.

"So I grabbed the son-of-a-bitch's hair"—he made a short upwards pass with blade—"and here it is."

I looked closer and saw the sprinkles of dried blood and the sickly white flesh.

"Know what I'm going to do with this?"

"No. Hang it from your belt?"

"Better. I'm going to make a mask that looks just like the punk, attach his hair and mail it to him."

Around seven-thirty at night we saw a string of lights that indicated Watson Lake. The bus rolled up to the depot which was in a service station–snack bar. There was an empty car outside with, of course, the motor running. Inside a woman could be seen opening up, switching on lights and the coffee pot to greet the passengers for their forty-five-minute layover. Arthur and I trudged through the snow having to lift our knees like cartoon Italian soldiers. I bought him a beer to make up for the vodka he had given me, and no sooner were we seated than we were joined by a man I recalled meeting in Whitehorse nearly twenty years before. Arthur knew him too, a squat, thoroughly bald fellow who used to help operate his father's drinking establishment before going Outside to play hockey.

"I've been in this bar for three days and nights and you're the first guys I can relate to."

Immediately he started to talk about his hockey career and how malevolent forces had conspired to prevent the success to which he was entitled.

The man's breath smelled like he'd spent all three days and nights eating sausage sticks from the box on the bar, and gobbling down those hardboiled eggs that floated in murky liquid in the huge jug that might have been there since the beginning of Alcan road construction.

Arthur tried to ignore him, saying something to me about carving, about other native carvers whose work he admired.

But the white man had been listening. "So, you know Willie Joseph, eh?"

"Yes." "You a carver, too?"

"Uh huh."

"You as good as him?"

"Maybe in twenty years. Why do you want to know?"

"Well, look. I own this condo in Palm Beach in Florida. If I had some good native carvings to sell down there I could make me and some natives rich. You interested in coming down there? Can you get Willie Joseph to come? I'll set you up in a place and you can turn out work. But listen, eh?"

"Yeah?"

"You'd have to work hard."

The man couldn't by now focus his bleary eyes but he still knew the order of things.

"You couldn't be drunk all the time."

He went on, letting us know, or letting Arthur know, that he was enlightened as hell when it came to relations between the races. He'd always dealt liberally with the innumerable 'drunken natives' he encountered in his father's bar.

"I've always been good to you people," he added, nodding his head at Arthur.

"You mean," Arthur said, staring hard at the man, "you've been good to Russian people or to Indian people?"

"Huh?"

"Well," I interjected, getting up from the table. "It's time for me to check into my room."

"A lot of Yukoners don't like you people. I'm not one of those but ..."

Arthur shot me a parting look, his lips twisted like he was suppressing laughter, malicious laughter.

I had a sudden flash of intuition, and knew what Arthur was trying to tell me: "Too bad this one is bald."

The next day I got a ride into Whitehorse and a couple of weeks later when I was done with my business, I caught a ride back to Watson Lake where I met a truck driver with a wood lot twenty kilometres from town. He was due to drive south in a couple of days with a load of logs to drop at Hazleton in North Central, B.C, and he offered me a lift. In the meantime I stayed in a cabin near his lot and by a small lake, more like a large pond but also called Fox Lake, same as the much larger one near Lake Laberge.

We went to B.C. not by the Alaska Highway but Route 37 through the Stikine mountain range and past Dease Lake. Nearby is Mt. Bedaux, named for the man who blazed a trail for an Alaskan Highway back in 1934. There is also a Fern Lake commemorating Bedaux's wife.

In the lodge at Dease Lake were two young fellows from Paris, France, who frankly admitted to being awed at their surroundings. One said to me, "But it is a long way from the sixième, non?" (by which he meant the 6th arrondissement, 'the Latin Quarter,' in Paris).

At Hazleton I got a ride to Vancouver on a twelve-seat passenger plane. While waiting for the plane a woman from Alaska told me, "I hope the pilot's not an Indian. They say that Indians can't fly planes."

But the pilot was an Indian and he got us to the Big Smoke unharmed.

So many memories.

Not too long after *Rough Road* was published, still living in Ontario, I got a magazine assignment that led to a couple of special experiences. First, I traveled to geothermal fields north of the resort of Whistler, B.C., and climbed Meagre Point, one of only two dormant volcanoes in Canada.

The approach to the mountains was across fields of boulders, many larger than a man. I stayed in a guide's cabin; there were no resorts then, only a motel or maybe two.

From Meagre I carried on to the Yukon, to search for traces of a village called Grand Forks that had grown up by the creeks in the Gold Rush years near Dawson. It's not even mentioned in most histories of the area yet at one time there were ten thousand people living in Grand Forks.

It wasn't until I reached the Yukon that I met a Canadian who'd ever heard of it, but when I got to the site, by following the river and the creeks, I encountered two German couples who not only knew all about Grand Forks but had come all the way from Düsseldorf to see what remained. And all that did remain were a few gray and warped boards, a couple of tin cans and a spittoon.

Back in 1981 *The Globe and Mail,* Canada's national newspaper, ran three excerpts from the newly published *Rough Road to the North.* There were plenty of letters and media attention, the latter mainly because of things I had said about Dawson Creek, British Columbia. Two of the letters, however, led to close friendships.

I had described a certain lovey-dovey scene between two women in the Alaska Hotel and Deluxe Evolutionary Café. The owner of that establishment who at that time called himself Charles Lux wrote to the *Globe* assuring its readers that displays of that kind of affection would never have occurred in his joint.

The same excerpt quoted a barber/hairdresser, a newcomer in town, who lamented that most of the local women resembled "lady loggers."

It seemed like half of Dawson Creek wrote in to chastise the big-city journalist who had merely dropped in for a few hours.

The mayor and the city director of Dawson Creek brought photos of their wives and daughters to city council meetings and displayed them, the photographs, at press conferences and on television.

The barber/hairdresser denied making his comments, and one official was quoted in the papers as saying that should I ever come to Dawson Creek again, I'd find a "necktie party" awaiting me.

It all worked out for the best, however. Charles 'Lux,' whose real name is Charles Kux-Kardos, and I met up a couple of decades later and are now good friends living only fifty kilometers apart, practically neighbours, on B.C.'s Sunshine Coast.

Not too long ago a woman in the building where I live lent me some books that had belonged to her late husband. One of them is called *Slipping the Lines,* the adventures of a man called John Rowland, and this fact relates back to the first edition of my book, to one of the excerpts and a scurrilous parrot named, of course, Polly, or at least the bird was known as Polly until it was discovered he was really a Peter, mostly known as Pete.

In chapter ten, I tell the story of Tagish Charlie buying his hotel at Carcross and about how Polly/Pete was left to him by the sea captain who drowned; Pete lived until 1972 perched in there cursing at all humans except children. It liked to watch television and bite anyone who introduced a digit into his domain.

This story annoyed one reader who wrote to the newspaper saying it should be ashamed, especially since the *Globe* was the country's paper of record, to publish such lies and nonsense.

Lo and behold, a reader actually came to my defense, maintaining that everything I had said about the parrot was the truth as he had heard it back in the thirties and, what's more, he was reminded of that nasty bird every day of his life when he looked at his right hand that was missing an index finger. Polly/Pete had done that job.

Ten years later I was living in Kelowna, B.C. and writing a weekly column for the *Courier* newspaper. One day I got a letter at the paper from a man asking if I was the same fellow to whose defense he had come via the *Globe and Mail*'s letters section years before. It was John Rowland, who invited me to call and to come see him at his home on the shore of Lake Okanagan. "We can look for Ogopogo"—the legendary sea creature that lives in the lake's deep waters.

We drank gin and tonics and John told marvelous stories about his adventurous life. He'd traveled widely and lived all over the globe. He'd made a lot of money during the years as a traveling salesman. His favorite place was the Yukon where he first ventured in the mid-thirties to sell magazine subscriptions, particularly the newly published *Newsweek.*

John told me about calling at trappers' cabins and mining camps, traveling mostly by shank's mare or canoe as there were no roads in those days. John said he sold a subscription to just about everyone he met because they were so isolated and lonely.

Well, I left the Okanagan Valley to do some traveling of my own and this put an end to our sessions 'looking for Ogopogo.'

Another ten years went by. I had moved to the Sunshine Coast and I was invited to read poetry and tell stories at a place in the city of West Vancouver called the Rose Cottage. The lady who called asked if I knew a man called John Rowland. I had forgotten the name but when I got to the cottage, the host took me aside to whisper, "Not only do you know him but you were pals together. That's him in the first row."

She indicated a raw-boned old man in a suit that was much too big for him. There was nothing to remind me of the fellow I had sat with by the lake, except there was something mischievous and familiar about the eyes.

I began to recite and he began to heckle me in a good- natured way. He'd yell for me to read more stuff about the Yukon. Some of the people in the audience didn't think this was very seemly. I started back on him and he laughed. At one point he shouted a question, "Did you ever date the lady known as Lou? Or how about Klondike Kate?"

The former was old Dan McGrew's "Light-o' love" in Robert Service's poem. The latter was a dancehall girl who hooked up with Albert Pantages, who became a great theatre magnate. They started out showing the new 'flickers' in a tent in Dawson and she staked Pantages when he wanted to build his first theatre. Meanwhile Kate wowed them with her lascivious dancing.

One day Panteges disappeared. When next Kate saw him he informed her that he was now married. She sued him and they settled out of court.

Lately there has been an attempt to prove that this woman was not the real Klondike Kate, and to whitewash an incredible woman's reputation. This politically correct version maintains that the real Kate was a self-sacrificing nurse, always bandaging wounds and ladling out free soup, and generally acting saintly.

This flies in the face of the memories of all the sourdoughs who witnessed the real Kate's dancing and sampled her wares upstairs at the Occidental Hotel.

I reminded John that Lou and Kate were before my time and it must have been he who went out with them. To my surprise he allowed as how he had been a special friend of Klondike Kate (who lived until 1972).

After the show John threw an arm over my shoulders and we walked out together. He'd always had an eye for the opposite sex and now he cast it on my companion. He complimented me on my good fortune, then went off toward home with his broken old man's walk.

IT IS BARELY A YEAR AGO as I write this in 2018 that I traveled with my old buddy Brad Benson to the Yukon.

A lot has happened since then. Brad died and I became very ill so the whole experience seems suspended in time, some other, long gone time.

We wanted to drive north from southern British Columbia but forest fires had closed all roads through the interior of the province, so we flew to Fort St. John only to find that there were no buses north.

So there we were, two septuagenarians hitchhiking to Whitehorse. We got our first ride just a couple of minutes after sticking out our thumbs. This from a young couple who lived in the area and were going for a post-church drive.

They were cheerful and optimistic and seemed perfectly at home with themselves and with this Peace River country. I wonder what they thought of us.

The next ride didn't come as quickly. We stood by the side of the Alcan for hours with our thumbs out, what old, old timers called goosing the ghost. There were very few cars and you no longer got rides from truck drivers, there being stricter insurance rules and 'security' issues.

An attractive lady from Penticton, B.C. in her forties took us a hundred or so kilometres up the road to a service station where she was meeting her son. He was a road crew worker and had gotten her a job as a 'flag girl.'

He didn't bat an eye when his mother got out of the car with a couple of rough-looking, by now old men.

They let us off at Pink Mountain and we repaired to the dining room. I remembered the very same tables from long ago, thick slabs of wood that had been highly varnished. They still wore a thin skein of shininess forty years later.

That night we slept at a workers' camp in the bush, the foreman letting us have a couple of small rooms in a construction trailer.

In the morning we were able to get a local bus into the old fur-trading centre of Fort Nelson.

In the evening we went to a pub where a woman was giving painting lessons to a dozen students. None of the drinkers paid them any mind. We stayed at a motel near a dried-up swimming pool and in the morning caught a bus to Whitehorse.

A couple of afternoons later, sitting at an outdoor table at a coffee shop in downtown Whitehorse, I looked all around trying to absorb the changes. Whitehorse resembled a sprawling, suburban town in Alberta. Getting off the bus at dawn I was totally disoriented. I didn't know which way to turn when I left the station, this on a street I had walked a thousand times.

There were vegetarian restaurants and shops selling scented candles; other places offered aromatherapy and shiatsu.

The Taku was long gone and so was the Capitol ('where miners meet'). A few locals I met hated the passing of the old establishments; only the '98 was left, unchanged.

In there we met a giant-sized young native man who told of his unrequited love for a white girl who might be in later. He too bemoaned the changes in the old town.

As for the rest of the establishments where one might sip a beverage or two, they were all fern bars.

Whitehorse was too depressing, and the next day Brad and I took the Husky Bus to Dawson City. The woman driver and I exchanged 'Don't-I-know-you?' looks.

It turned out we had been nodding acquaintances in the West End of Vancouver in the 1980s.

Just a few minutes out of Whitehorse Brad and I got talking to the fellow across the aisle who had plenty of questions about the Yukon. He told me I looked like "an old Yukon rounder."

I thought to myself, if I had stayed after that first trip or any of the other, earlier ones, that was exactly what I would have become. Part of me, a big part, regretted that I hadn't.

Stuart Newton was a tall, lanky Englishman in his late sixties. Recently retired and emigrated to Canada, to the city of North Vancouver. Stuart Newton was in a position to do whatever he wished and the first thing he had wanted to do was visit the Yukon, particularly to see sights related to the poems of Robert Service.

Newton could recite whole poems, even the later non-Yukon things like "Ballad of a Wage Slave." But at first it was all moiling for gold and the strange things done.

Not long after we started talking, I said, "If you look out your window and through the trees, that brightness you see is Lake Laberge. Yes, we are on the marge of it."

Later in Dawson City, I would direct to Stuart to the Bank of Commerce where Service had worked.

We talked about writers who'd been to the Yukon, and Stuart said he admired poets who'd actually worked, done manual labor, particularly in the outdoors.

He said, "My second favorite poet is one of those. Well, you've probably never heard of him, named Peter Trower, known as the logger poet."

Brad and I looked at each other and laughed. Peter Trower had lived in our town and had been a close friend to both of us. I used to visit him at his apartment at least twice a week for years. He'd telephone me nearly every day. We had the same tastes in music—jazz and rhythm and blues—and we had both spent years working.

Pete would reminisce about characters he'd met in the woods and the Vancouver skid row hotels where loggers went when they'd been paid off.

But for the last few years, Pete had been in a nursing home, suffering from Alzheimer's. Just recently he'd gone into the hospital. Stuart had looked him up and introduced himself and from then on went to visit Peter nearly every day until Peter passed away just a few weeks later.

In Dawson City the three of us were walking along Front Street and I pointed out the branch of the Canadian Imperial Bank of Commerce where Service had worked.

"As you probably know Service wrote his poems while working for the bank in Whitehorse, and one night there he was, writing in a back room. A guard took him for a bank robber and shot at him. Luckily, he missed but it gave him ideas.

"Service," I added, "probably would have liked the story of Dawson City's most famous bank robber."

It wasn't some old desperado with a load on come to town from Bonanza to rob the bank and generally wreak mayhem. No, it was a young fresh-faced kid who'd walked the four blocks from where he lived in a double-wide trailer with his mother. At least, he was fresh-faced in the seventies during his 'crime spree.' He was always unarmed and unfailingly polite, although to be honest about it, he was a little simple.

He appeared at the bank with a paper bag and implored the tellers to fill it with paper money, which they did. The boy then left the bank and went home where he put the paper bag under his bed.

There was never any panic among the tellers or no one ever pressed the alarm button. When business slowed down, and if it wasn't break time, a call was put in to the local RCMP.

When a Mountie answered, an employee would say, "He did it again."

"Okay, we'll try to get around there later today."

Eventually a Mountie appeared at the young fellow's home.

"Oh, no," his mother would groan.

And the Mountie would nod. He'd go in the house and back to the young man's room and give him the required, though futile, lecture which always ended with the young man vowing to never rob the bank again.

But two or three weeks later there he was with his paper bag.

He might be still doing it for all I know.

Brad and I tried to avoid the hordes of tourists. There were dozens of people of the type you meet in supposedly out-of-the-way places throughout the world. All dressed the same, sort of self-consciously sloppy with tousled hair, and you expected at any moment they'd produce a guitar and start singing an early Bob Dylan song.

They never went into the Westminster though, which was still the same as it always had been, and the pink exterior paint was probably the same coat it had gotten in the seventies or maybe even the 1890s.

The owner had done portraits in oil of all his regulars, and these used to be fastened to the wall behind the bar so that often the living regulars would sit facing themselves.

Most but not all of the paintings were gone but some still hung around the joint. The owner was still alive but too frail to come to work. I regret not remembering his name, and regret not having the wherewithal to buy a few of those portraits.

Dawson City had changed but the town is unique and transcends the modern inroads, as if Moosehide would always be there to look down and make sure it was okay. It was in Dawson that I felt most strongly that Yukon thing, felt it more powerfully than one did even in the middle of the wilderness because the looming mountains and forest somehow made one seem special yet insignificant at the same time.

I thought of my very first trip to Dawson City when I went to the old age home because there were still a couple of people, a man and a woman, who had been around town during the fabled Gold Rush of '98.

The man wasn't able to remember things but the woman recalled how crowded the streets were and how there were 'ten boys for every girl,' and one man had sprinkled gold dust in her hair.

We wanted to travel up the Dempster Highway to the Arctic Circle but without our own vehicle it was nearly impossible. The rental companies didn't allow their vehicles on the Dempster because it was too rough. We could have chartered a minibus but weren't about to pay $3,500 each. We could have tried hitchhiking but as the car rental man said, "There's no traffic."

A couple of days later, Stuart bid us goodbye and Brad and I rode the Husky Bus back to Whitehorse on the first stage of our journey south to home. We had the same driver, and she and I talked whenever we had a rest stop. I asked her if she ever would consider going back, leaving the Yukon for the 'Outside.'

She looked me square in the eye and said, "No fucking way."

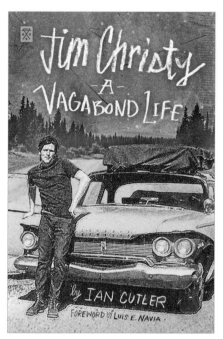

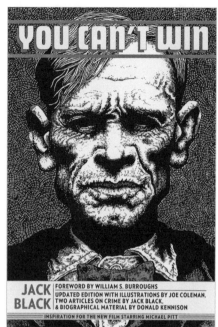

 TRAMP LIT SERIES
WWW.FERALHOUSE.COM